Date Due

EXPLORING MUSIC

EXPLORING MUSIC

ESSAYS BY
ERNST KRENEK

Translated by
Margaret Shenfield & Geoffrey Skelton

NEW YORK
OCTOBER HOUSE INC

90036

First published in Germany as 'Zur Sprache Gebracht'
by Albert Langen · Georg Müller, Munich, 1958

© Ernst Krenek 1958
© This translation Calder and Boyars Ltd 1966

First published in the United States 1966
by October House Inc
Second printing January 1968
LC 66-15268

CONTENTS

The essays in this book were translated by Margaret Shenfield with the following exceptions: *On Writing My Memoirs*, *The Ivory Tower* and *Composing as a Calling* are printed in translations supplied by the author. *That Noise Called Music* and *Conversation Past Midnight* were translated by Geoffrey Skelton.

ON WRITING MY MEMOIRS

WRITING memoirs is quite a commonplace thing. Presidents and valets, prime ministers and starlets, princes and paupers are equally intent upon communicating 'inside stories', things which they believe the world does not know, but should know, because such knowledge would complete or rectify the picture of events which at the time of their happening were known incompletely or in distorted fashion.

When I decided in 1942 to start writing down the story of my life, I had something different in mind. The book on which I have been working off and on ever since and which at this time covers my life up to 1932 on well over a thousand pages, is not meant for publication. The Library of Congress has graciously consented to receive the work in safekeeping and will, according to my instructions, not open it for inspection until fifteen years after my death. The first four volumes of the manuscript were recently delivered to the Library, and the subsequent sections will be deposited there upon completion, with similar restrictions.

The immediate reason for my embarking upon that time-consuming enterprise was my discovery that I began to forget a great deal about my earlier life. I ascribed it to the fact that through my emigration to America in 1937 my life was bisected into two phases which seemed to hang together less and less, especially when after 1939, contacts with Europe became scarce and after 1941 stopped completely. The reality of my life in this country was so strong that it obliterated memory of my previous life in Europe as soon as this memory was no longer fed by reminders in the shape of letters, or otherwise.

At first glance it looked like a fairly simple proposition: write down what you can remember. However, when I was engaged in research for my opera *Charles V*, I had learned a few things about the dialectics of history, and thus I expected complications to arise sooner or later. They made themselves felt rather sooner than later. Being cut off from Europe as I was when I started my work, I was unable to consult any records such as diaries, letters, or other sources of reference. I had to rely solely on my memory, which, in a sense, is perhaps how memoirs should be written anyway. Of course, I would frequently hit upon blank spots where no amount of hard thinking would supply the missing links. Should I then give up the whole project and wait until I might be able to retrace my steps with the aid of references? This did not seem to be advisable, as at that time I was under the impression that Europe was lost for ever, that I would never see it again, and that all records of my earlier life left behind over there would be destroyed in the course of the war. In fact, it is due to mere chance that they were not destroyed. A bomb hitting three hundred feet further southwest than it did would have done the job. Under these circumstances waiting would have entailed forgetting more of what I still knew, without hope of recapturing even that, let alone what was already blurred by the passage of time. Thus I decided to go on with the work as well as I could, aware of the fact that my account of past events was not accurate in the strict sense.

But, then, what is the strict sense? The statement 'I left Vienna on November 26, 1929, at 8.20 p.m., arrived in Zurich on November 27, at 10.12 a.m.' may be accurate according to scientific standards, as it may be verified by consulting witnesses, inspecting the records of the sleeping car agency, checking railroad time tables, hotel registers, and the like. But it is meaningless in terms of the story I want to tell. If I say, however—all this being a fictitious example—that it must have been some time in the fall of that year that I took a trip to Zurich because I feel that certain tendencies showing up in a work that I conceived in the following year should be ascribed to some experience or impression which I could not have had unless I had been in Zurich and met there such and such a person, my statement, problematic as it is in a pragmatic sense, is meaningful because it tries to establish an interpretative context. The fact that my memory on that particular point is blurred is not any longer an annoying deficiency, but it becomes the vehicle of my efforts to impart meaning to the meaningless, to allude to Theodor Lessing's famous title of his philosophy of history.

From the point of view of psycho-analysis one could argue that my forgetfulness at that particular moment is due to repression engineered by my will to establish that particular interpretative context even at the expense of pragmatic accuracy, which process causes the lacunae in my memory. Both ways of looking at it amount in effect to the same. At any rate, my attempts at interpretation obviously have something to do with the frame of mind in which I find myself while trying to remember circumstances of the past. In other words, what I try to write down about the past, is conditioned by my present state of mind.

Thus it may seem that the document which I leave to posterity is more revealing with respect to the period in which I am writing than to those periods with which it deals. But the reader would never know anything about those periods unless he will view them with me through the medium of the period of my writing. In his *Doctor Faustus*, Thomas Mann has beautifully elucidated these conditions of historical writing by projecting the reminiscences of Serenus Zeitblom against the background of the period in which this fictitious biographer of Adrian Leverkuehn is compiling the history of his idolised friend.

Whether Napoleon lost the battle of Waterloo because his map did not show a certain ditch in which his horsemen got caught, as a recent advertisement of Rand McNally's wants us to believe, or because of a sudden inspiration visited upon that usually pedestrian cavalryman, General Bluecher, or because of any other reason, we shall never know, for the whole affair, tremendous as it was, has reality only in the reports written about it, and they contradict each other. In this respect the humblest artistic effort is superior to the most glamorous deeds on record. The terrific and tragic battles of the Peloponnesian war are irretrievably lost in the stream of time, but Thucydides' report on them lives on, not so much because those battles are so important for us that we are still eager to read about them, but because of the inherent significance of what he had to say. The earth-shaking deeds of Julius Caesar are nothing, but a poem of eight lines by Catullus has today exactly the same total presence which it had when it was written. One might say that it is timeless, but by the same token it is history, for it has been alive for two thousand years.

Be that as it may—why should I expect anybody to trudge to Washington fifteen years after my departure from this world in order to find out what I thought I had been doing while still alive? In my little book *Selbstdarstellung* (Atlantis Verlag, Zurich, 1948) I indicated as the main reason for my writing this huge autobiographical book my conviction that some day my musical work will be considered far more significant than it is at this time and that then people will try to discover what made me tick. It is curious that commonplace things are of no importance when they happen except as material for gossip, while later on they become of absorbing interest. Undoubtedly no one except his close friends paid any attention to Franz Schubert's life. Today O. E. Deutsch's *Schubert Reader*

9

is a deeply moving document because it reveals how the great little man spent his every day.

However, my main motivation for writing down the bulky story of my life is of course my pleasure in doing so, although many pages of it cause me as much torment as I would feel undergoing a severe psycho-analysis. I have always had the strong desire to step outside of my personality, as it were, and to watch myself critically do what I was doing. Writing up my life only partly satisfies that desire, for no matter how successfully I may step outside of myself, I still remain within. My writing still belongs to what I am doing, and as such it will be judged. What I really would like, is to become someone else and, fifteen years after my death, walk to the Library of Congress and look up what I have written. This, however, will not be granted. Yet, I may hope that I then will be in a position of having all insight and knowledge that a human being can desire, without consulting any terrestrial papers.

1

A PUPPET PLAY

DURING 1926 a 'society of art-lovers' was formed in Kassel. I started the idea at a gathering of several fairly active people, and out of the discussion that followed there emerged a project that nobody had foreseen at the beginning. The unusual thing about the organisation was that we did not establish a democratic or parliamentary society with a committee, a secretary and so on; the four or five of us just put forward a programme for five evenings, presented it to the public and watched to see how many people would apply for membership, at a very reasonable fee. As emerged later, this fee was much too low, for as time goes by the actual cost of this kind of thing always exceeds what has been anticipated. On the other hand, if we had charged high prices nothing would have come of the whole undertaking in a town not inclined to spend anything much on cultural endeavours. In the end we had a group of a hundred and twenty people, and this seemed to be a basis on which we could risk the enterprise.

Four lectures on current art-problems were planned and for the fifth meeting I wanted to offer something rather more stimulating than dry words. Somebody suggested a small stage-performance, but this struck me as unsuitable because in any case the theatre, as such, was not much in demand in Kassel, and because there was no sense in doing something with improvised means and an unsuitable locale, so that it would turn out inadequate and amateurish and the best performance we could manage would only be everyday fare in a really good theatre-

11

building. This led me to the idea of putting on a puppet play, something which I knew did not exist in Kassel. It could be done with relatively simple resources and without terribly high costs, and it seemed very attractive to the public. I chose Marcel Achard's *Marlborough s'en va-t-en guerre*, a play which I had been trying to get on to a real stage—unfortunately without any success—ever since I had seen the first performance at the Théâtre des Champs Elysées in Paris in 1924. Apart from the fact that I liked the piece, it had the advantage that I would have to adapt it for the puppet stage, and this is the only thing that attracts me to creating performances of any kind.

At first I thought of calling on members of the local art academy to do the numerous artistic and craft jobs that were necessary, for it was our society's aim to set in motion all the possible artistic forces in the town and the academy always complained of being neglected and slighted; but as on other occasions, we found that this plan was to fail largely because of the narrowmindedness, selfishness and crankiness of the people assembled there. Then it came to my knowledge that S., our scene-painter, not only was an enthusiastic puppet-lover but had himself worked for several years as a puppeteer in Cologne. I had a very slight knowledge of the subject, which I had picked up when in 1924 I had got to know the Swiss Puppet Theatre through my friend Grubler, but it was almost nothing, as I soon found out, and I was glad of this assistance. Unfortunately, this too proved to be inadequate, for after many vain attempts to prevail on Mr S. to teach the young sculptor who was to make the puppets something about their construction and mechanism, it emerged that he had forgotten all the essentials. Our rescue came by a very circuitous route. I had planned at first to have the performance in the ballroom at Wilhelmshöhe Castle, a most beautiful room which, like many other places in Kassel, stands empty and is complained about,

12

though plans for their use always meet with stubborn opposition. We saw over the building and found that a lighting mains would have to be brought over from the castle. A man who played an important part in Kassel's fine arts, supported us and was always helpful and full of ideas, even if he was not always very active and could be unreliable. He sent us to the necessary electrician. To our great amazement, he told us that he knew exactly what was needed, as he had once fitted up just such a puppet theatre which must be somewhere in Kassel. We promptly set about getting hold of the man it was made for and found him a naturally gifted person who was not fond of work and had been reduced to very poor circumstances. He told us he had the puppet-theatre and would set it up in the place where it was stored so that we could take a look at it.

It was in a dismal, neglected area: the building was an abandoned warehouse that seemed to have contained a workshop at some time. Although various objections were raised, I had the theatre hired for our performance straight away, for the first cursory glance told us that, even if it was simple, a new one would have cost much more money than we had and could not possibly have been finished by the date arranged. Best of all, however, the puppeteer could let us have various puppets which the sculptor could use as models.

Now the actual work began, and I saw how a project which in itself seems trivial takes on unsuspected and almost unmanageable proportions when you try to create it from the very beginning. It emerged that nobody really knew much about it, but I did not lose heart, for I had learned that you can master anything once you start actively doing it yourself.

First of all I began rehearsals with the puppeteer's existing puppets, because the ones for our play were not yet ready. The following principle gradually emerged: the nature of puppets is half mechanical—their bodies move according to the physical laws of the materials they are made of, but these movements are caused and controlled by the man who pulls the strings. So the expression that the puppets' movements represent is the one the puppeteer chooses to give it, translated into a lifeless substance. Herein lies the strange, human-inhuman magic which is the peculiar charm of the medium. For the person who devises or performs puppet-plays the attraction is the limitless number of ways the puppets can be constructed and used for expression; they can have the most fantastic forms, figures and movements, although everything is quite simple and easy to construct.

Our first puppeteer was joined by a few assistants. They were all extremely willing people, some very gifted, who had been deprived of an ordered life and systematic work by some peculiarity or misfortune. As a result there was something superficial, improvised and absent-minded about their performances too. This was partly due to the way the puppets were constructed; they were much too light and meagre, and the people at the Kassel school of commercial art had made them in a rather mannered style, so that it was much harder to keep them still for an instant than to move them. Consequently I took care that the puppets now being made should be heavier and more stable. You cannot work out any characteristic and expressive movements when the puppets are constantly wobbling backwards and forwards, although it must be remembered that there is always something succinct and terse about puppets' movements; they are really confined to a few recurrent basic types, so that you have to be very sparing with them.

Puppets' expressiveness is dependent on their construction, that is, the way their main centre of gravity and the centres of gravity of the individual extremities are distributed in the puppeteer's hand through the strings. The puppet's body is made out of cloth stuffed with seaweed; inside it there is a simple wooden construction consisting of a slightly longer piece of wood, which roughly occupies the position of the spine and two shorter cross-pieces attached to the ends of the longer piece and roughly equivalent to the shoulders and pelvis bones. The head, which can move in every direction, is attached to the top crosspiece with a screw and ring, and the legs are nailed on to the bottom crosspiece with small strips of material, so that they too are movable. Whether, and how, one introduces knee-joints depends on the kind of movement one has in mind for the puppet. The most practical way of imitating nature without getting a grotesque effect proved to be a hinge-joint, which prevents the shin coming forward in a ludicrous way when the puppet kneels, etc.; but this is a rather complicated construction. But we also had puppets with completely stiff legs (military types) and female ones without any legs at all; with these last it is important to have solid enough skirts, so that the puppet does not collapse into a formless heap too easily. If this arrangement is used the skirts must be cut like a barrel, the same width all the way down, so that in curtseys, for example, they bulge outwards instead of falling in, thus giving the impression of knees, although there really are none. In clothed puppets the arms, which can and must be more mobile than the legs, are best made in such a way that the sleeves are only very lightly stuffed with cloth, etc. in the upper arm, so as to create a minor centre of gravity there; otherwise strings are only attached to the wooden hands. The head, being carved out of wood, is of course the heaviest part of the whole puppet, and this contradiction of nature has to be counterbalanced by placing the strings correctly. In carving, one should beware of too great sculptural intricacy, because, for one thing, details are lost and only make a muddled, complicated effect, and, for another, each puppet's facial expression remains the same from beginning to end of the play. It takes a great deal of artistic

15

sensitivity to give the head an expression which is typical of the total character and fits all the changing situations of the play, without itself being able to change. Sometimes the back of the head is hollowed out so as to compensate somewhat for the weight-displacement. If so, a wig of wool or some similar material must be added, but this does not give a good general effect and always looks trivial and small-scale. At all events it looks better when the head is all wood; light willow or maple is used.

Which parts of the puppet are moved and how this is done depends on the way the strings are attached. Four strings are used mainly to keep the figure in an upright posture: two are attached to the temples and two to the shoulders. They also make the figure turn sideways when their upper points of attachment are swivelled. If they are lowered the whole figure sinks, but if you want to make just the trunk bend over you must attach a string to a point somewhere around the small of the back; the upper end of this string remains stationary when the shoulder strings are lowered. The two strings which give the main expressive movements are those attached to the hands. Here one must take care to have the centres of gravity in the right place so that the palms remain turned inwards and the backs of the hands outwards. If one wants leg-movements one has to attach strings to either the toes or the heels, The heel-strings are necessary to pull the feet backwards, in kneeling for example, the toe-strings for step-movements and some ways of sitting down. In any event, one can add as many strings as one likes in this way, and the figure can make any movement the imagination can devise. I have seen puppets with concertina-type necks which could be extended indefinitely, puppets with independently swivelling goggle eyes, tiny and especially attractive animal puppets, and so on. At first I was disturbed by the fact that it was impossible to simulate natural walking movements. Our puppeteers found that this movement was not missed; but I am still convinced that something suitable could be effected with some small mechanism—a small eccentric wheel or something of the sort, which would be automatically set in motion when the puppet moved from one place to another. The walking-movements of jointless legs attached to alternate levers made a good effect in a puppet consisting of four officers. With their shared body (striped after the fashion of a Prussian sentry-box) and an aggregate of five arms and eight legs, they were something of a novelty in any case.

As it is often necessary to lower one system of strings while keeping the other up, the strings must be kept separate from one another in the puppeteer's hand. For this, one uses a so-called 'controller', a wooden construction exactly corresponding to the one inside the puppet's body. With this very simple gadget all the necessary effects can be obtained, one lot of strings being fixed to one crosspiece of wood and the other to the other. One hand holds, raises and lowers the controller and regulates the puppet's all-over movements; the other hand works the hanging strings which govern the expressive movements.

In performance the ideal situation would be for the puppeteer to work the strings and say the lines at the same time. With enough practice the hands' string-manipulations would directly replace acting gestures—I have in mind a kind of psychological substitution which would give a particularly convincing performance. But, of course, the puppeteers would have to be excellent speakers and know the text by heart. As our puppeteers had neither the intellectual powers nor the acting experience to be able to deliver Achard's highly subtle and pointed dialogue, the speaking and string-pulling functions had to be separated. Then, of course, we had to have an excessive number of rehearsals, for the puppeteers had to get used

17

to the text, which I read over and over again, and to make the desired movements 'by ear'. The whole thing went much faster with the real speakers, members of the Kassel State Theatre. After a few rehearsals singly and together, the reading was done as I wanted it, and the ensemble with the puppeteers was achieved quite easily because I had drawn the speakers' attention to various places where the puppets' movements meant they had to wait or adjust in some way. I had the speakers sitting on either side of the stage so that they had a clear and easy view of it over their books. All our arrangements were rather primitive, and one could easily think of many improvements, but at the time they could not be carried out for lack of time and money. For example, there was no entrance through the centre, and the theatre as a whole lacked depth, but to improve this would have meant building on a large section at the back and made it difficult for the puppeteers to move from right to left—they moved on a gangway behind the curtain or backcloth at the back of the stage. But even as it was, it worked and made a very good effect. At the performance the experience of ages was confirmed: once again the spectators entered into the spirit of this miniature world so thoroughly that they lost all sense of the real size of the puppets and in the end felt them to be life-size, against their better judgment. This is the almost uncanny magic of puppetry, and it could be used with ghostly effect to illustrate the deeper significance of the puppet-show. In the course of the action, its threads and those of the puppets would become so entangled and intertwined that no rational solution would seem possible: then a puppeteer's hand, absolutely gigantic in the magic puppet-world, would reach down like God's hand and give the play an arbitrary ending. It would have to be done at the end of the play, for it would shatter the illusion.

18

2

A FEW WORDS ABOUT
JOHANN STRAUSS

JOHANN STRAUSS may be called a product of his age, unlike Franz Schubert, with whom he is often displayed by the window-dressers of Vienna's musical parnassus. Schubert is a huge tree with very firm roots and a top reaching right up into the sky, whereas Johann Strauss could be compared to an iceberg with only a sixth of its volume showing above the water it floats in. Consequently it is important to learn about this medium that supported him, if he is to be assessed correctly. His music is very much Gebrauchskunst (workaday art), in the solemn, disagreeable language of today (as though it were some kind of novel invention), and its intentions are altogether collectivistic—that is, it exists in correlation to a particular society.

Strauss lived from 1825 to 1899 and his work was done mainly between 1848 and the end of the century. Now for Vienna, and Austria in particular, 1848 was a turning point of great importance. The age before this point, known as the pre-revolutionary or Biedermeier period, was a time of very concentrated intellectual and cultural prosperity in Vienna. Metternich's system of censorship, which is supposed to have had a muzzling effect, did not in fact harm any real intellectual product much; only the believers in a liberal economy blow up the petty, ludicrous tricks of this system, which missed their marks by a mile, into a despotism of bigots and a kind of latter-day Spanish Inquisition. In reality Metternich was concerned to keep the underdogs as far as possible from politics and everyone might well have been grateful for this at bottom. Political activity, being unpopular with the authorities, was replaced by an enormous interest in art and love of the theatre which embraced all circles of society. We can only be astonished and envious when we see, from accounts of performances of Nestroy's works, for example, how familiar a relatively large section of the population—Vienna probably had about half a million inhabitants at that time—must have been with everything to do with literature and the theatre. In fact the town was so saturated with culture that even Schubert's new creations, which were as daring as they well could be, were enthusiastically accepted and understood by tradesmen and suburban schoolteachers.

The second half of the century brought a marked change. With increasing industrialisation, liberalism—the rationalisation of affairs and minds—gained ground. As the outlying suburbs were incorporated in the town, their native elements were also exchanged: for example, the waltz which had been developed by Johann Strauss the Elder and Joseph Lanner in the better suburban inns, such as Domayer's Casino in Hietzing and others, became the music that accompanied fashionable and aristocratic occasions and even penetrated the imperial court ball. This was the ground in which Johann Strauss the Younger grew and developed, and the waltz—the Strauss waltz which accompanied the life of Viennese society for fifty years, just as Bach's cantatas accompanied the Sunday worship of the Leipzig churchgoers—was his true life work.

From being a local, indigenous creation, the waltz gradually became the entertainment of enormous numbers, a thing of universal currency. It is really to Strauss that the credit is due for the fact that it remained at a high level of artistic perfection: this is the real achievement of his genius. For it is well known that the wider the audience is, the lower the level is likely to be and the danger of degeneration is strongest with 'commercial' music, meaning basically the kind that is chiefly designed to be played in places where nobody listens to it and it is only meant to provide a pleasant background noise for the flirting and gossip. The Strauss waltzes have no equal for rhythmic subtlety and variety or melodic richness. And then there are the introductions to the waltzes—childlike, yet in their very naïveté unusually imaginative, inventive and often quite daring—which try to suggest the meaning of the totally irrelevant title in just a few bars.

Strauss's operettas are really only an opportunity to use this art of waltz-writing. This is really the great difference between Strauss and Offenbach; it is always ignored on the numerous occasions when the obvious comparison is drawn between the two, because this usually does not get beyond the banal observation that one was a Viennese and the other a Parisian. The important thing is that Strauss was a waltz-composer and Offenbach a dramatist. Offenbach, directly supported by his librettists—his instincts led him to the right kind—has the gift of making contemporary local types so transparent that you can see through the outer shell of absolutely flat, typically obvious reality to the most basic features of human behaviour. The 'bubble bubble' chorus in *La Vie Parisienne* is the archetypal frenzy of the human race, translated into the transient material of the Second Empire. The second act of *Die Fledermaus*, on the other hand, is the gorgeous apotheosis of the champagne-tipsiness a society might justifiably enjoy after producing incomparable material achievements and bringing the 'good, old' Austria to the verge of ruin. Here one can already sense a little melancholy and fear of destruction which gives the genre picture greater scale.

The Gypsy Baron represents an ill-advised step into a worse future: it is the beginning of the cultural scandal of later Viennese operetta which dominated the beginning of the twentieth century and whose last horrors and excesses have still not died out. Sentimentality reared its ugly head along with a distasteful folkloristic arrogance; this led to the habit of seeing the non-German peoples of the Austrian monarchy as curious, laughable exotics, good enough for the Thaddädl clichés of operetta—a habit whose consequences we are still suffering for today. All the same, everything is wrapped up in a phenomenal wealth of beautiful music which will always give these works a certain life even when they themselves are no longer interesting as memories of a great period—brilliant, sad and very strange.

FROM *JONNY* TO *OREST*

A T first glance the transition seems absolutely impossible. How does one get from a more or less naturalistic contemporary piece in which the whole technical magic of the present day is deployed, to venerable classical material from Greek mythology which obviously demands 'noble simplicity and silent grandeur', as Winckelmann put it, in form and content? Now, from the point of view of contigents the transition really is rather difficult. Perhaps it will seem more plausible if I try to show the connection between these works as I myself see it.

At this juncture I need not point out that the technical miracles in *Jonny* were not really miracles, but just perfectly ordinary objects from everyday life (a telephone, a loudspeaker, a train-engine) and as such were merely the props necessary to present a drama growing out of the every-day life of the present. They are never presented as values in their own right or symbols, but only as vehicles of a dramatic action which cannot do without them for both internal and external reasons. The external reasons are obvious: the loudspeaker on the terrace of the mountain hotel solves vast dramaturgical complications, the car rattling its way through the streets saves long, intricate scenic detours—but these things in themselves are not conclusive: if necessary they could have been done in a completely different way. There are also internal reasons for them. Showing these completely soulless machines is the shortest way of demonstrating the antithesis which inspires the piece—the antithesis between man as a 'vital' animal, and man as a 'spiritual' animal—as incarnated in the diametrically opposed figures of Jonny and Max. In this sense Jonny is actually a part of the technical-mechanical side of the world; he reacts as easily, as gratifyingly exactly and amorally as a well-constructed machine. His kingdom is of this world, and as a matter of course he is the one who gains mastery over life here below, over the visible globe. He is in direct contrast to Max, who, starting out from spirituality, never comes to grips with the problems he is set by external life, which is so attuned to vitality today. Only at the moment of greatest peril does he decide to assent to life—but at this moment the opera ends. We shall never know what he does after this, because I did not know when I wrote it. The confrontation between the two spheres of life never takes place, Max's and Jonny's paths never cross, apart from the one fleeting encounter in the car which does not lead to any intellectual result. The duality of the world is presented without being brought to any crisis.

In *Das Leben des Orest* I try to show something different. The duality of life, the tragic divergences between the vital region and the spiritual region, the technical and the cultural, which naturally exist at every period but can be shown particularly clearly in the material of the present day—this aspect was less important to me; the important thing was the ambivalence of the single individual, his ability to go from one pole to the other: in short the bridge between Jonny and Max, instead of the gulf between them, as in *Jonny*. The overall impression, the broad lines of the Orestes of the Greek myth seemed to contain this journey from one pole to the other: his savage murder of his mother and Aegisthus, growing out of the stifling, inhuman swamp of blood-revenge, was the point of departure of the development: the destination was his emancipation through the gods' grace and his entry into the more airy regions of thinking humanity. Accordingly the murder had to be moti-

24

vated as the aberration of an able person and backed by a corresponding history: he was repressed by his ambitious father and, after first being destined for the famous sacrifice, escaped this fate and lived the licentious life of a vagabond for ten years.

After the catastrophe comes the return: the curse of his dying mother is only the outward projection of his inner collapse. In Tauris he encounters the pure, simple courage shown by Iphigeneia in the face of her own sacrifice and for the first time he becomes aware of higher possibilities in life, after so much experience of horror. On the long wandering journey to Tauris he is ennobled and takes on a better humanity which at last demonstrates to him the plan of grace of the deity. The unusually copious and complex details of the myth had to be fitted into this primary sequence of ideas, which I have briefly outlined here. For this reason I obviously had to be very free in my use of motivations, connections, omissions and additions. Above all, everything that was bound up with the period and the ancient Greek origin of the material had to be jettisoned. The opera takes place in a very concrete and colourful period, but it is not otherwise identified.

I have really already answered the question of why this idea is not presented through present-day material, if it so closely related to the idea behind *Jonny*. The answer is that at the moment I see more gulfs than bridges in the present period and so to present the bridge I had to go into the past. Whether I shall succeed in finding and portraying a synthesis for our own divergent age in a future work is more a question of my own future experiences than of direct artistic purpose. What I have attempted in *Orest* must be understood in this light, as one station on a lengthy journey which I have tried to explain here. In the final analysis all we ever try to do is to get closer to goals which are more or less distant from us.

DARIUS MILHAUD

THE car has driven up the steeply rising highway that leads to Aix-en-Provence; it has passed Marseille's last giant blocks of flats, faded but not depressing, with between them the last glimpses of the Mediterranean glittering up in the dazzling light of the afternoon; and now it goes out through two steep hills, as through a gate, into the Provençal landscape. In a certain self-evident sort of way it is classical or, as in Poussin, something of whose picture-world lives on here, heroic. You feel it cannot have been so long since the Greek colonists arrived here and the greater and lesser gods that escaped out of their bags and boxes dispersed and settled in the fields and hedgerows. Over there, under those three cypresses, where some sort of rustic shrine seems to gleam yellow, perhaps an ordinary satyr will make his appearance, and we will know him for a satyr instantly, even though today he may choose to go about disguised as a post-man or a glazier, like the angel Heurtebise in Cocteau's film *Orphée*. And so the many brightly-coloured petrol pumps along the way do not disturb the natural landscape which in the cate-gorical, unequivocal clear air of our Austrian alps is often so easily spoiled by man-made objects. This is a dreamland of short circuits; everything is ambiguous and secretly everything fits together perfectly—the huge shape of the Corsican emperor who threatens you with 'Brandy of Napoleon' every half a mile or so, fits in with the dusty agave by the wayside, the eternal blue sky with the smelly little Ford that pop-pops its way crossly down the road between endless flocks of sheep. Soon we come to the town of Aix itself, with its canyon-like streets cut deep into the wonderful Empire rock-faces and every now and then, on the shady side, a black cat slinking away. Here, too, is the inescapable square with its four rows of plane-trees—the Cours Mirabeau, I think—where the life of the town takes place, the antediluvian cars of the provincial French, who are not snobbish about being up-to-date, bouncing happily around the greengrocers' shops and open-air cafés, barking like so many little dogs, beneath the gaze of the legendary Bon Roi René in stone. He lived somewhere around the twelfth or fourteenth centuries and yet they talk of him as though he had only just died. Probably not much has altered substantially, and what is called 'progress' is still man's servant here, in a way we have long ceased to have any idea of.

If you follow the boulevards, which indicate the old town walls, you soon reach the property called L'Enclos. Near this old, characteristic country house, under the central clump of trees in its large garden, as beautiful as it is useful, there lies on a chaise-longue a jovial man, always ready for a funny anecdote, a man who looks enviably like the archetype of royal leisure, of the only life worthy of a human being on this earth. This is Darius Milhaud, undoubtedly one of the most industrious composers of this century.

His relationship to all these features of the landscape, to the whole nature of Provence, is certainly one of the most powerful mainsprings of Milhaud's creativity, and it shows clearly from his works. Needless to say, I have no room to analyse these works in their entirety or even list them all, but I would like to mention one or two of the most important stage works.

The peculiar timelessness of the Frenchman's historical consciousness (which Friedrich Sieburg makes so plain in his outstanding book *Gott in Frankreich*) shows most in the works based on classical material. To the French the past is not exactly

28

something complete in itself, distant, perhaps even something that alienates us of the present. Their attitude towards it is neither the opposition of the young to the old nor the demand that historical accuracy must be preserved when the past is being portrayed. What is past is, so to speak, totted up and constantly carried forward onto the next page. People do not consciously distinguish whether a thing is a hundred or a thousand years old: in so far as it exists it is a possession that must be conserved and must enter directly into present-day life as much as a newly created object. It is in just this way that Milhaud treats the classical legends he uses as material: in *Malheurs d'Orphée* Orpheus is a village barber, Eurydice a girl from a wandering tribe of gypsies, and what happens could happen in any century in the mountains of Les Baux or the region of the strange village of Les-Saintes-Maries-de-la-Mer in the Camargue, a place of pilgrimage for the gypsies. This is perfectly matched by the music, which aims at a 'folk' type of rhythm and melody.

It is much the same with the three *opéra-minutes* (*Europe, Ariane, Thésée*) which Germans are inclined to take as ironical because of this strange attitude to the subject-matter (unfortunately among some German art-critics *anything* normal and natural can only be taken as a joke). Only the last of the three little works, *Thésée libéré*, is in a comic vein; no Frenchman would think of the other two as jokes. The ancient myths are used for particular purposes, just as one might use Louis XVI furniture, without any intention of laughing at them.

The same closeness to nature and the national character—nothing whatever to do with 'restoring' the national heritage in a folkloristic, philological sort of way, but a real source of artistic creation, as it should be—occur in the gigantic *Orestie*, which embraces the whole of Aeschylus' trilogy in Claudel's version. Here, of course, Milhaud is aiming in general at a different, more monumental style than in the previously mentioned works, and in part he uses different means, as we shall see. But there are still many signs of his close bond with the timelessness of the people and country. The colossal finale of *Les Eumenides* is not only a composition on a huge scale, such as few men have succeeded in managing, but also an overwhelming, unequalled picture of the boundless, torrential exuberance of southern life, a formidable thousand-part counterpoint which you can occasionally feel around you when you stand on the ferry in Marseille harbour. *Christophe Colomb* may be considered a continuation of this line; and here too, though on a much higher level, there is the same southern national character and meridional nature, monumentalised in subject-matter from a timeless past that is near to the present. The salvation of the hero comes at the end of both *Les Eumenides* and *Christophe Colomb*; it is more acute and typically French in the second work—the action through which Columbus can achieve happiness, despite all his many serious mistakes, is an intellectual action. America is an extension of the horizon of man's knowledge and in comparison with that the question of increasing the stock of happiness in this world, or even the fact that the majority of the people of the period lived in unhappiness, is of very secondary importance. (The idea that an extension of knowledge finally serves to spread the Catholic dogma and only then takes on meaning and significance comes from Claudel, but Milhaud used it very happily to heighten and 'spiritualise' his own statement. For after all, this triumph of Catholicism, too, is in effect a victory for the pure, more refined Latin spirit over the extravagant, grotesque, barbaric darkness of heathen Mexico.)

Then there is another group of works which have quite a different character and yet share the same characteristics: *La Brebis Egarée* and *Le Pauvre Matelot*. These treat material which belongs absolutely to the present day—as though it were time-less. The scenic aspect dominates in *La Brebis Egarée* and the local-character aspect in *Le Pauvre Matelot*. It is rare for music to suggest landscape as evocatively as *La Brebis* conjures up the limitless, dream-engulfed summer plains at the foot of the Pyrenees. For example, Pierre's description of the classroom, misty in the brooding summer heat, his monologue, in which the dangers that he himself sees in his friend's wife's letter of temptation are strangely, dreamily intermingled with the accidents the farm machines cause—he can see them through the window—all this is a model of the most accurate evocation of landscape created with extreme economy, like a Rembrandt etching which gives the infinity of the horizon in two strokes. Compared with the glowing tones of the local colour and the intensity of the inner life of the few characters in this chamber-drama, modern props, as such, fade away into insignificance; just as *Orphée* could take place today, so *La Brebis* could be set in any period one chose. And yet the everyday objects and words give it a strange charm that is moving because it brings everything so pitilessly close.

Le Pauvre Matelot, with its full-blooded, strong colouring, is something quite different; here everything depends on a rich vein of folk-character—it is a stage ballad. Java, which begins the piece and recurs as a refrain throughout, proves this. Actually such 'folk-songs' can hardly be localised; their 'country' is really an attitude, a quality of mind, a sadness and melancholy wildness rather than a territory. Their locale is as difficult to determine geographically as those of sea-shanties which resound with every coast and bay and blend together to make up the vocabulary of the wanderer. But just because of this, the opera's theme—a horrific, anecdote taken from the local section of a popular newspaper—takes on the proportions of timeless tragedy.

In the main Milhaud's technique follows two compositional principles—the tonally cadenced periods of tradition and a sort of heterophony tending towards polytonality. At first these two techniques are still very closely related; later they diverge more clearly, to form new units. Harmonically speaking, *La Brebis Egarée*, with its ninths and whole-tone scales, often shows its derivation from Debussy very clearly; in it there are, on the one hand, plain, simple periodic constructions in which the harmonic relationships are governed by their importance in the cadence and used dynamically for lengthening and shortening, and, on the other hand, long stretches of the ostinato technique that was later to become characteristic of French music to an almost oppressive extent; the orchestra repeats a melodic phrase or a repeating harmonic complex and only the voice part indulges more or less freely in a parlando following the melodic line of speech. On rare occasions the periods grow into larger, strictly constructed and articulated forms, or the ostinato becomes the basis of a unified sort of passacaglia. It is all the more remarkable that despite this renunciation of clearly recognisable structure there emerge patterns which are always temperate, most delicately weighed and balanced, and often of amazing dimensions (the church scene, Pierre's monologue on the promenade in Burgos, Francoise's letter scene, etc.). Here is another admirable example of the uncannily certain instinct which the French have for all human proportions, so that they know exactly how to avoid monotony in a passage built out of the most sparing materials and, so to speak, without any external attractions, simply by manipulating very trifling deviations and nuances; whereas far less economical works can become monotonous much sooner, simply because the funds are allowed to run out much earlier.

Later the 'period' technique of tonal cadences separates off clearly; it predominates in the ballet music and above all *Le*

Pauvre Matelot, where it is dependent on the folk-song element. From then on the ostinato technique is used chiefly for monumental presentation, particularly in *L'Orestie*. It develops in this way. Instead of a motif or chord-complex being repeated continually, the ostinato figure is picked up and imitated by another part a few bars after its entry, while it continues in the first part. But since the imitation is not related to the key of the first part but imitates the interval-leaps absolutely, the second and later parts starting on different notes are all in different keys. Often the ostinato consists simultaneously of two or three corresponding parts or a chord-type complex, and then the imitation also extends to these patterns, giving so-called polytonality—the consistent co-existence of several keys side by side (not a mixture for colouring purposes!). This alone would be a very feeble principle—and when, in imitations, it becomes a cliché it is unbearable—if it did not happen that, particularly in *Christophe Colomb*, the heterophonous results of this technique are once again related to a basic key, giving a great deal of charming ambiguity in the notes of melodies and chords. If used alone or even predominantly, this method, which appears in the great intermezzo in the last act of *La Brebis Egarée*, may have its drawbacks, but Milhaud, piling up parts and chords with ruthless consistence, achieves climaxes of overwhelming energy and power, particularly in *L'Orestie* and *Christophe Colomb*.

This technique pushes a constructive principle to its extremest extreme, so that you sometimes feel that the creative process must have included such a consideration as: 'I'll just see what will happen if I ruthlessly pursue this fourth-figure or that sequence of triads through twenty bars.' And it expresses, among other things, a strong love of fun, which also figures prominently in Milhaud's life. His house, filled with old-fashioned furniture and family photographs by suburban photographers, is a kind of chamber of horrors, the exhibits being fantastic, tasteless objects from every chance country—particularly bottles, which Milhaud collects with a rare passion and success. He is also madly in love with his old picture postcards showing highly varnished couples in front of twilit pools with flat backgrounds, or idiotically smirking pink ladies saying 'Ne m'oubliez pas!' and similar abominations from the lumberroom of the nineteenth century. It is no love-hate that binds him to these things, no surrealistic feeling of horror at the deadness of this aesthetic world, but the primitive southerner's honest fondness for the highly coloured, absurd clichés which give pleasure to simple-hearted sailors and housemaids. A gin bottle shaped like an umbrella may be objectionable aesthetically, but to the Marseille harbour workers, for example, who are not so conversant with the finer points of applied art, it is an original imaginative creation of the finest order, and reflects eternal beauty and art better than a Beethoven symphony, which they do not understand—and consequently it is better than a vessel shaped on the most unexceptionable scientific and aesthetic principles. This throws a light back on Milhaud's work, so far removed from all artiness, and always taking the most direct route to the heart of its subjects and so to the hearts of its listeners. His music is always good, warm, sincere, like the man who created it, for which reason it has something—indeed a great deal—to say to us all today.

5

COMPOSING AS A CALLING

In one sense composing, like all art-creation, ought to be called a 'vocation'; not only does it demand special gifts but the imperative feeling of being 'directed', the irresistible urge to work in art, undoubtedly plays a large part in it. It is quite possible to accept this without blowing it up into a solemn approach that is often ludicrous. Very little more need be said about this aspect of composing, especially since experience has shown that the strength of the creative impulse is proportional to the size of the talent, the capital on which it can draw, and the intensity of the power with which it is used. It is more usual for the creative urge to be greater than the talent—as demonstrated by the pathetic prolificity of many dilettantes—than for a man who *could* create to be hamstrung by a lack of drive, by laziness. If he thinks this is the case he is, at best, unconsciously deceiving himself as to his creative powers. He who can, composes.

But composing as a calling in the second, more down-to-earth sense, is another question altogether, and in an age to which sociological and practical considerations matter it is not only important but quite feasible to look at composing in this way. In the context of the economic system of today, which is largely liberal and based on the principle of free competition, a calling's right to exist, from the material point of view, depends on the law of supply and demand. If a calling does not pay—that is, if there is not enough demand for its products—it is, economically speaking, unproductive and is bound to die a natural death. In other words, if a man wants to compose string quartets professionally and finds that these 'goods' are not 'wanted'—that the profits from selling string quartets do not cover the costs of the business (meaning at the very least the author's living expenses while doing the work)—then he must give it up. I deliberately put it in these brutal terms because at the moment we are not very far away from this state of affairs. Despite all the fine talk about 'spiritual food', etc., music is not something that a person absolutely needs, to keep alive, but a definite luxury article—and when times are bad, as they are now, people will only smoke cheap cigars and will not go to concerts at all. And at the present time, in particular, as I have mentioned elsewhere, music has to face competition from cheaper and more convenient types of distraction which fall within the same range of interests as art and so are prejudicial to it. If professional composing is to make sense, then, two factors are necessary: first, the economic situation of the music-lover must be such that he can afford the luxury of music, and second, this purchasing power must be matched by an interest in music.

In the past there were two ways in which a composer could live, at least partly, on his work. He could be an employee of a church congregation and provide functional music for it (Bach), or he could be attached, more or less tightly, to a private patron who gave him commissions. He might be engaged specially to carry out definite compositional duties, like Haydn, or merely given regular support by one or more rich music-lovers who did not directly influence his work (Beethoven).

What has happened to these relationships? As far as functional music is concerned, there is now only one customer who really counts: the popular entertainment industry in all its manifestations, from the dance hall to the cinema and private gramophone, and it is no secret that producers of this music make a very satisfactory living from their work. But there is a marked difference between its level and that of the functional church music of the seventeenth and eighteenth centuries. In my opinion, however, there is no demand for 'functional music', 'Gebrauchsmusik', of any other kind; 'functional music for music-lovers' is a contradiction in terms, for the idea of loving automatically excludes that of using (that is, using it for some purpose outside itself). If music-lovers want music made specially for them, then I do not believe they are music-lovers; they could and should first apply their love to the wealth of splendid music that was written without them in mind.

But patronage, by prosperous individuals or organisations, is in a bad state too. Private patronage has as good as stopped altogether—partly, it would seem, because rich people no longer want to spend their money on musicians, and partly, no doubt, because owing to present-day forms of swift and limitless publicity it is no longer possible for patrons to have the sole (or at least special) rights in compositions which their eighteenth-century counterparts could claim to a very large extent. For this reason painting is preferred as an object of patronage: a patron can become the sole owner of a visible and unique work which in certain cases can even be used for speculation and in that way bring in more money, which is not possible with musical works.

Of organisations only the radio has emerged as a patron on a considerable scale, and even then its patronage is sporadic and handicapped to a certain extent by the special character of the reproduction it gives, which does not exactly stimulate the composer's free inspiration. In a certain sense publishers (although, admittedly, hampered by the poor economic situation of today) and performing rights societies act as patrons, in that they balance things up, as it were, by using profits from other things to subsidise works of moral and artistic merit by composers who are coming off badly, from a matter-of-fact estimate of their material results. Occasionally objections are raised to this 'alms-giving' economy—and they are certainly not without justification, where the system is concerned. But my feeling is that there can never be any perfectly satisfactory system in human affairs, because one always has to reckon with the human beings who operate it. This is just as true of the organisation of a state as of a society of authors or a haberdashery counter.

The doctrine with its articles is only a sort of vague, external outline (this kind of thing must take some form or other); from the ethical point of view the results must always be ascribed to the talent and character of those who use the mechanism. This, no doubt, is also the answer to the proposal often put forward by socialistic schools of thought—that art should be declared a national necessity and artists supported or aided by the state; perhaps many who hold this view are thinking of Athens in the ancient world. But they tend to forget that at its zenith Athens was strictly feudal in its organisation; the free citizens, governed democratically but strictly limited in number, devoted themselves to a life of leisure, while the work was done by a much larger number of proletarians who had no rights whatever. If we wanted to re-create this state of affairs we could no doubt rightly demand first-class cultural achievements from the state, and get them, but I have an idea that those who believe in state aid for art would not be quick to accept these conditions. Moreover the idea is open to the objections that the defining of an artist would be handed over to a bureaucratic commission which would have to judge the worth of each individual case, and finally that the state, as the wage-giver, might justifiably exercise an influence on the type and tendency of the art it was financing. Of course, a private patron may well demand that I dance to his tune if he pays the piper, but nobody is forced to do either; it would be highly immoral if the executive body, obliged to suppress unpopular tendencies, were to be identical with the employer. (Many states find sinecures for certain artists, making them attachés in embassies or something of the sort, and perhaps this is the most humane solution, because it takes most regard of the individual; the drawback to it is that it usually only applies to 'successes', who do not need it.)

Whatever the rights and wrongs of the case, all these makeshift aids and stopgaps are hardly enough to make composing into a living in the bread-and-butter sense. I have described the state of affairs under free competition. There are very few cases —and those probably of limited duration—of composers creating a work which makes no concessions to low standards and yet guarantees its author's material security for a time. It follows, then, that the composer needs to have a secondary occupation and he can think himself lucky if it does not develop into his main occupation.

Now the question is: which type of money-making occupation is most advantageous to the main aim, composing? Possibly some job which has nothing to do with music and art would be most suitable, for the discrepancy between intellectually free creation and financially dependent activity would be less palpable when the two spheres did not overlap. Of course, the composer would have to be something that would demand as little time and intensity as possible, perhaps a post-office clerk in the country, a signalman, a customs officer or something of the sort (I mean this quite seriously). On the other hand, it will be found that when the composer has once entered the so-called 'public' life of music his earning occupation will move in a different rhythm from his artistic occupation. As a composer he will need to travel about and stay in various places for considerable periods, which his 'bread-and-butter' job will not always allow, and this will create all manner of conflicts. In general, it is a natural corollary of the swift and extensive publicity of today that the engagement books of even moderately 'public' figures get so full up that they have little time left for other things, even if only because they need that spare time as a bulwark against the onslaught of publicity. So the composer will probably prefer to look for a job that has some kind of connection with music, because two activities within one sphere are easier to fit in with one another. No doubt he will choose a teaching post, a conductorship or something of the sort, according to his special gifts (let us hope!).

On occasion a second activity of this kind can actually be very beneficial to the main aim, the development of his creative powers, by giving the composer the necessary practical experience and knowledge. The greatest importance should be attached to these aspects in the composer's musical training too. It is not just a question of his knowing about double counterpoint and other theoretical tricks; he must be master of the whole range of his art, for he exists to create it and so occupies its key position. I do not mean the basic-craft aspect—he does not need to be able to play the bassoon himself—but he must know all the parts and their functions from his own experience. Over and above this, his general culture cannot be universal enough, for one can only create out of a very deep and wide fund of human experience, never out of a technical academic expertise. Perhaps the music schools should lay more stress on this in their teaching programmes, so that 'general studies' would not be merely a despised necessity, to be shirked if at all possible, but a direct intellectual aid. To take one example, the 'history of music' taught to budding composers should have quite a different content from that taught to orchestral students. On the one hand it should be viewed in a much wider context of general, and above all cultural, history, and on the other hand, there should be much more special emphasis on details of compositional technique—dates and anecdotes being given a very secondary place—so that it would actually complement the composition lessons. Moreover, in dealing with the history of music, there is often a tendency to overdo the idea of development and see everything only as a transitional stage leading to further achievements. Thus at best one learns how Monteverdi 'enriched' forms, how he 'extended' techniques and 'perfected' harmony, etc., but nothing is said about the special, imperishable, absolute value of his creations. But here again it does not depend on the system, but, to an enormous extent, on the teachers. So it is impossible to give a generally valid answer to the question: should a person study at an academy or with a private teacher? One can learn more about composing from a conversation with a real teacher—even a conversation about the economic policy of the U.S.A.—than from five years in an academy; but on the other hand nothing can replace the academy with its splendid learning apparatus always available for practical use.

6

NEW HUMANITY AND OLD
OBJECTIVITY

As far as the German tongue reaches, or rather as far as newspapers printed in German are read, their readers are being
disturbed, to a greater or lesser degree, by perpetual discussions
about a crisis in art, especially in drama and music, which seem
to share a common fate at the present. This crisis is viewed
in the most widely different lights. Some think that not enough
is being produced, that there is a shortage of geniuses capable
of producing really enjoyable and convincing work; others
wonder whether films in general or perhaps talkies in particular
are harming drama and music; sometimes it is radio that is
having a bad effect on art; sometimes sport is held responsible
for the decline; sometimes the bad economic situation is supposed to have had a restrictive influence on the enthusiasm for
art which, it is assumed, would otherwise exist. There is no
end to the discussions, inquiries, investigations, admonitions,
eleventh-hour warnings, appeals and so forth, and any public
figure has lost count of the times and places at which he has
been urged to express himself strongly on the crisis. The remarkable thing is that this crisis is always taken to exist in drama
and music only; I have never read an inquiry into the crisis in
painting or sculpture.

If we go into the causes of this, the true character of the so-
called 'crisis' emerges. Painters paint pictures, art-dealers sell
them or do not sell them; this covers the whole activity involved in visual art. But behind and around music and drama
there are enormous organisations, organisations containing

thousands and tens of thousands of people, indeed indirectly an enormous number of industrial and commercial activities of all sorts are involved in music and drama and an incalculable number of people earn their living through them, largely from public money—and this is enough to make the object of all the activity, the arts of music and drama, the centre of general interest. The real heart of the crisis, and the reason why it is so interesting, is a question of economics and this alone explains why there are so many discussions about a subject that nobody really cares about, as I shall show. Strangely enough some inhibition still stops this age from saying, quite simply: 'The commodity of music is not selling any more: let us convert the concert halls into swimming baths, or anything else that is profitable.' Instead people try to veil the commercial aspect, which is somehow repugnant to them, and debate the inner condition of art, tacitly hoping that some mysterious process will make it able to find a market once again.

To keep up the commercial analogy, the reason an article does not sell well is because there is not enough demand for it. Our crisis-observers usually penetrate as far as this but most of them do not appreciate the special reasons for the low demand in our particular field. It is not true that there is less understanding of music today than in the 'good old days'. Possibly even the reverse is true, for thanks to an almost all-embracing educational system many more people learn something about music than in any other age. Nowadays we look back with admiration at the way in which J. S. Bach became such a perfectly valid symbol of his age, the way art and culture were one and the same thing in such an age. But we forget that the 'culture' of an age as we see it from afar consists only of its highest peaks—the valleys between them have vanished into the darkness of the past. We know very little about what interested and occupied the great mass of ordinary people of the time; we only see what the cultured did, because only they took care that it should be handed down—and there were no more of them then than now or at any other period. But it is true that for them art had what may be called an intrinsic value, if we understand it correctly, and this will be one of the most important points of my thesis.

By art's intrinsic value I mean its ability to appear an obviously necessary element of certain points of human life, something which the public demands of its own accord and is offered spontaneously. This is the point where one can, with some justification, consider art and the culture of an age as related. If we are looking at art in the context of cultural history we obviously have to ask what an art means in the particular culture concerned, but also how one can judge from the culture of an age what kind of art had an intrinsic value, in the sense I mean, in that age. We must bear in mind that a culture is something collective and art is something individual. By culture I mean a higher total picture that emerges from the many conflicting individual lines, while each manifestation of art is unique, unrepeatable and, for these very reasons, raised above everything determined by its period. The intrinsic value of this unique and individual thing is the extent to which it enters the current, typical, collective culture and becomes part of it. If this is to happen often there must be a living convention, something the great cultural epochs of the past had in a very high degree. And by living convention I mean a naïve, unselfconscious but unerring, immanent limitation of its intellectual channels.

In old music, for example, this can be seen very clearly in the fact that for a very long time virtually no harmonic or other external musical means would be altered, yet the music did not become poverty-stricken or stereotyped. The early masters did not restrain themselves from making changes because they were uninventive, or changes were forbidden; they *could* not change anything because they did not *need* to change anything. All the force of individual imagination went into making-up and re-making more or less the same material, in ever-new patterns, in the service of ever-changing intellectual purposes. The advantages for the cultural collective are obvious: the constant quality and immutability of the material, to which the art-consumer is born, just as he is born to all the other intellectual realities of his culture, saves him from having to use his powers of apperception in this direction, and all his ability can be turned to the purely artistic aspect, the quality which is independent of the material, and questions of intellectual substance. The stronger the convention and at the same time the more alive it is—that is, the more elasticity it has, the more it is able to follow the turns of the individual mind with conventional means—the better off art will be in such a culture.

The golden ages of art have always been periods such as I have described. Think of Greek antiquity, when for centuries visual art and poetry constantly played variations on a group of unchanging themes, the mythological material that was inexhaustible and, of course, astonishingly flexible. All Attic tragedy has only one subject—the long-known mythical themes handed down tirelessly and unceasingly since the mists of pre-history; there are only a few essential variants, which are more like re-interpretations and exegeses, and so belong to the actual process of artistic creation. There was virtually no attraction towards the whodunit type of curiosity which works on the tension produced by wondering how the plot will end; consequently all the attention could, and indeed had to, be directed to the way a perfectly familiar outcome was reached. The public of the day must have had an extraordinarily lively and subtle feeling for values which the present-day public can hardly even conceive of!

The painting of the Italian Renaissance shows us another outstanding epoch of the same kind. Again and again artists, the same artists, repeated their madonnas, their crucifixion-scenes —sacred subjects which had been fixed since time immemorial and indeed dogmatically confined, so that their actual substance could not be changed in the smallest degree. And yet it is absolutely true that, as Jacob Burckhardt observed, these masters reached a peak of directness and freshness in constantly repeating these traditional themes, while they often seem much feebler, much more outdated and conventional in the bad sense, when they tried to be original as to their material.

Shakespeare is another example of this phenomenon in the field of literature, although he could not take his themes either from a still living mythology or from a religious convention. All the same, hardly one of his plots is original; they come from the stock of literature which happened to be in vogue in his period and circle, or from history, which was, apparently, enthusiastically studied at the time and so well known to many. The artistic end is the same: the suspense that might derive from an unknown plot is not allowed to distract attention from his main concern—the presentation.

On quite a different basis, pre-revolutionary Vienna provides an instance of a self-contained theatre-culture in which a genius like Nestroy could develop. He never invented anything, but almost exclusively 'arranged' plays that were already traditional and indeed were often being played simultaneously in their original form in neighbouring theatres. Only in that way could he be sure that his main concern, the How of the writing, could make its greatest effect. Here again the prerequisite was that the public should be homogeneous and familiar with the essential bases and artistic values which have disappeared altogether and for good.

What sort of an age do we live in now, if we take these

cultural elements as points of comparison? What is important sociologically about these 'good' periods? First of all there was a circle with its external boundaries more or less clearly defined, a Society, so to speak, for which *alone*, or virtually alone, art existed. The artist himself needed neither to create nor to seek this society; he really belonged to it *a priori*, for there was nothing else apart from it. Whatever social rank he himself assumed—and he might well be equated with the cook, gamekeeper or gunsmith—it only emphasised how much he was part of society and necessary to it. Secondly: within this clearly-defined circle there was an intellectual convention which limited the material of art most beneficially. People were not interested in perpetual change of theme, but in the greatest possible differentiation of artistic presentation, and moreover they were able and trained to pick up such subtleties and feel them, without having to go through an intellectual process. Most members of society were also prepared for this by themselves being amateur practitioners of one or more arts.

Here something must be said in favour of the much-maligned amateur or dilettante: he is the man who really carries on an artistic tradition and culture; he has an insight into the limitations of art because he is actively concerned with it, even if by definition he stands outside it and his centre of gravity is elsewhere. Added to this, the amateur has always enjoyed the instruction and guidance of a professional. The danger of amateurism is, of course, that this instruction can be bad, so that, instead of respect and insight, presumption and narrow-mindedness set in, for the amateur always has a tendency to think himself perfect when he has reached a certain level.

Our art-epoch differs from the others described, in that neither of these conditions—the limited circle and the living convention—exists any longer. Instead of the limited circle we have what is rightly given the ambiguous name of 'the general public'. The guilty party, to borrow a pregnant phrase from Burckhardt, is the ubiquity of all things intellectual, the fact, or at least the fiction, that all values exist everywhere. Here the revolutionary factors are applied science and the press, the latter being really only a necessary, though very marked, consequence of science's empire over the world. The characteristic feature of the applied science of the last hundred years—and this has become clearer and clearer at an ever-increasing speed over the last few years—is first of all that the invention precedes the need for it, so that applied science has long become a thing in itself, like art and pure science, growing, spreading, developing in its own right, without regard to whether and how people will need the achievements it offers. This would be all very well, even if it does contradict the very essence of applied science, which ought by definition to be an aid to living, but it also demands that it should be needed and so the fact that necessity is no longer the mother of invention produces the result that invention creates necessity. Naturally it is impossible to teach people to abstain from technical miracles when they exist, and so everything has to take its course.

The telegraph and telephone make it possible to hear an enormous amount enormously quickly about an enormous number of things, and this fact undoubtedly creates a situation where people do so, and the damage is already done. Once the idea of quantity, as a virtue, becomes rooted in culture (and applied science undoubtedly brings this in its train), it spreads like dry-rot and increases by feeding on itself incessantly. If people know they can know everything, they immediately want to know more. The press puts itself at the service of this news-apparatus, and floods the defenceless public with information. Intellectual inventions, wrung from the imagination with great effort, naturally have very little news value. Probably the best-known fact about the theory of relativity, the fact that has made the most impact, is that Einstein plays the violin; this after all, is hard news.

Nowadays the radio fills in the gap between the morning and evening newspaper so that there is not a moment of silence in which anyone might become conscious of a void, and there is even the television to relieve us of the trouble of using our visual imagination as we might have to when absorbing news through other media.

But much can still be learned from these things. On the one hand technology certainly surrounds us with a superabundance of apparatus on whose correct functioning we depend, although as non-technicians we have no influence whatever on it, so that our life becomes ever more complicated; on the other hand it constantly simplifies its internal methods with regard to the quantity and speed of production. Thus it soon becomes able to satisfy existing need, and then has to call on the services of advertising, this being the acknowledged medium for creating needs which do not really exist. But luckily even advertising can be done scientifically, so that there is no need to worry about its precision and effectiveness.

What is it most important for a man to be today? Christian, Jewish, nationalistic, radical, Communist, artist, soldier, paterfamilias, sportsman or what? None of all these—he must be a consumer. Frugality is a luxury nobody can indulge in any more, and the time is probably soon coming when one will not be able to afford not to own a car—or what will they do with all the hundreds of thousands of cars which, with improved methods, roll off the production belt every day? As everything makes its appearance masked as cultural progress, it is understandable that although last week nobody might have known he was missing the radio, today it is absolutely uncivilised not to have a set of one's own. But to be able to buy everything which is presented as an absolute, indispensable necessity people have to earn more, which means working more, producing more, selling more, and so this earning-owning mentality spirals ceaselessly upward in a continuous reciprocal process. Since each new invention puts wages into the pockets of legions of men—only, of course, so as to be able to take them out again for other inventions—no activity of this kind, however crazy, can ever be stopped once it has begun. However bad a talkie is, it must go on, for whole industries have involved themselves in it, and if it did not, what would become of the people working on it? They would cease to be consumers of motor-cycles, weekend cottages, silk stockings, vitamin pills, radio sets and football matches, and then other workers . . . and so on *ad infinitum*.

How does all this bear on the question of art's position in our age? People of today—the general public, that is—are smothered by a confusion of news and impressions. The enormous quantity distracts them, its content gives them a senseless hunger for facts and kills their imagination. At the same time they are compelled to need more and more externals and, in order to buy them, have to work more and more, and more and more pointlessly. On the average, then, the general public is a conglomeration of distrait, unimaginative and overworked consumers. You will say, perhaps, that other sorts of people do exist; of course I know this and want to show that these are the ones who matter. But this famous general public makes demands on art and so must be taken into consideration. For one thing, the general accessibility of everything that science and the press have brought with them has reduced differentiated society to a general mediocrity in which the theory is that everyone is equally far from or near to the intellectual centre. For another thing, art itself has attempted to compete with science by showing that what it offers is value for money; in part this is simply because so many material interests are in-

90036

volved in music and drama that if only for this reason it seemed desirable that they should go on existing and above all be conducted on a rational basis.

Now in music the age has found the art that satisfies all its needs—popular music. As far as its production and consumption are concerned it corresponds perfectly to the other present-day principles of creation and running. Production takes on a conveyor-belt system—each of the numerous operatives taking part in the process carries out only one 'repeated, thoroughly learned action' as they say in the collective contracts for a given category of industrial workers. We hear that there are refrain-specialists, verse-specialists, specialists in harmonising the half-finished product, others specially skilled in producing witty or imposing titles; there are others who do the rhymes and specialists in radio, salon, jazz and other orchestration who then put the finished product into its normal commercial package. It is rather like a cloth factory where at one end the wool is taken off the sheep and at the other the finished material emerges. But in this case the part of the fleeced lamb is played by the unconscious consumer.

This art is, of course, adjusted to the conditions of a large turnover; the goods are mass-produced, so that production-costs are lowered; the articles are almost interchangeable types so that you can get away with an unsubtle, dull feeling for the type and are not disturbed or surprised by individual traits; the material is easy to understand and the words satisfy the hunger for scraps of information in a particularly accessible field half-way between sex and sentiment.

But of course it must not be thought that this art is deliberately produced because there is a need for it, and that its creators could write differently if they chose. On the contrary, here as elsewhere the demand is created by the producers, for at bottom the public is indiscriminate, ready for anything. The writers cannot do anything else because they themselves cannot rise above this sphere and one cannot but be convinced that they are doing the best they can, for no artist can deliberately write below his real level. If anybody says he could just as well write symphonies as pop songs and only writes the songs because they pay better, he is lying, perhaps unconsciously, and ruining his character without improving his talent. Without any doubt at all, everybody always does the best he is capable of at the time.

The truth of the matter is that every society has its art, and the aristocrats of pre-revolutionary Germany had Beethoven because they valued intellect and perhaps even had some themselves. I am not saying that as a class they understood Beethoven, even approximately, or could have met him on an equal footing intellectually, but they valued what he did enough to spend time and money on it. Today this social class no longer exists; instead we have the general public and that procures what *it* wants to spend its time and money on. But since its aim is to be economical with both, the goods it gets are correspondingly low in value.

Now the really essential question arises: is it possible for art to go along with this social change? The answer is bound to be no. Since nobody can give less than he has in art, as I have said, those with too much to give drop out. The intellectual purchasing power of the general public is too small to be able to pay for the surplus. And to add all the individual powers together is of no use here, because at the entrance to art there is a turnstile through which only one person can go at a time, when he shows his ticket; parties do not get any reduction. Since the intrinsic value of art, which I mentioned at the beginning, is now determined by an illimitable number of people, only an art which suits the capacities of that huge number can have any intrinsic value. It is well known that in a majority, the standard is always set by the lowest and never by the highest, for the level is a line common to all and that is always the bottom line, not the top one.

Despite this state of affairs, attempts have recently been made, and more will be made in the future, to create an art, particularly an art of the musical theatre, which will fit the enlarged society as earlier art fitted the limited society—in other words to find a basis for an art that the general public could enter into and assimilate. In this connection I must mention my own efforts. They consisted mainly of including some parts of the rhythmic and harmonic elements of jazz in my works. The motives that led me to this now strike me as twofold. Firstly I thought that by using the jazz elements I might hit on an atmosphere which would fit the collective feeling of the age. As jazz music in practice enjoyed undisputed mastery and general validity, it seemed conceivable that from it one might derive an artistic means that after all belonged to the sphere of music, and so was capable of the most serious and intellectual development, while at the same time having a natural place in the life of modern man. This, I felt, might give me the possibility of saying something generally valid.

The second consideration was an internal musical one. As must be fairly well known, there has been a complete disruption of musical systems of organisation along with the democratic opening-up of the conventions of life. At first, atonality, which tried to replace these systems, extended the range of musical means to infinity, theoretically at least, so that today there is really nothing that is musically 'impossible'. Every conceivable harmonic combination can be produced at any time, without special preparation, and a new organisation from this quarter is not to be hoped for. So far, atonality has not proved particularly suitable for versatile dramatic presentation and in the circumstances jazz, with its stereotyped harmonic and rhythmic elements, seemed an effective protection against the

54

ineffectual ubiquity of all musical possibilities, because it offered a sort of new convention. But there was never any idea, least of all in my mind, of its being a complete substitute for every other kind of expressive world; only if that were successfully achieved would the product really deserve the name of 'jazz opera'. In my attempt, as in all the others I know of, jazz was only alluded to at the points demanded by the action; apart from this the harmony was coloured by its elements, thus guaranteeing the homogeneity of the whole and justifying the way I had deliberately limited the means—a protection against atonality.

Looking back on the results, one is bound to be aware that works of this kind were only connected with the general public 'atmospherically'—that is, by being reminiscent of the familiar pop-style—while their real artistic value remained irrelevant and obscure. Nevertheless it must be admitted that in this sphere the good is still usually more successful than the inferior, while just the reverse seems to be true of operetta, for example. The amazement and agitation I caused by showing a station and having somebody telephone on the stage have since died down, and there is not much point now in going into the pro-grammatic interpretations people read into these things. There have always been naturalistic operas, and the props, if they are no more than that, are probably the least important symptoms of an attitude of mind. From any moderately reasonable point of view, my *Jonny Spielt Auf* is one of the unhappiest examples to quote in connection with Neue Sachlichkeit, 'new objec-tivity', for although new objects occur in it they do so only as objects surrounding present-day people, without proclaiming any positive attitude concerning them. Nobody prays to the engine or lauds the virtues of the telephone; these things merely play a subordinate, functional role as props needed by the action, and there is no more reason why a present-day work should do without them than why a drama taking place in the past should do without the modern props of that age.

But there are other efforts along these lines which must be taken much more seriously; in them the essential thing is not just using daily objects for personal reasons, as in *Jonny Spielt Auf*, but assenting to everyday aims as such. Of course it is true that anything can be made into artistic material, but it is essential that the object should stand in a dynamic relationship to man. The object must release a feeling; to apply this to the complicated conditions of a theatrical process, the object must be an obvious vehicle of dramatic movement within the course of an emotional pattern translated into action. For example, the fact that there is a telephone means absolutely nothing artistically; however intensely the instrument is accepted, as it may be by many people, this cannot give any occasion for artistic creation. For even if you wanted to address a poem to the telephone you would have no choice but to gear it to man's use of the machine, its position in man's life; and to get the emotional content needed for the poem you would have to examine whether and how the fact of telephoning plays a part in the expression of man's inner life. Description alone is not enough, and even a list of all the component parts of an aeroplane would not add up to a Homeric epic.

On the stage the telephone can only be used as a prop, a characteristic feature of a milieu, as stage-coaches, distaffs, shepherds' crooks, spears and swords were features of other milieus, and no one milieu is *a priori* better than another. Nothing further can be derived from this—no theory, no aesthetic position, no dogma, nothing to gladden the heart of the philistine thirsting for knowledge. But the Neue Sachlichkeit I have criticised puts the prop in the centre of the picture and so reflects the situation described above—the fact that the technical devices created by man have long since become ends in themselves and reduced their erstwhile masters to servitude. Instead of machines serving us silently and exactly, and setting us free to find ourselves more quickly and easily, they get in our way and themselves become the monuments they have destroyed, for which we have such an ineradicable taste. The divine in man has been replaced by the fact that he can travel faster than a bird flies; and in the advertisements, the inventor of a new kind of engine rivals the creator of the world.

We now have the 'rhythm of the age' and so know all the less about the rhythms of music; we are bored to death with the 'tempo of the age', but nobody is allowed to fall behind. Now I conceive of a work of art as the intellectual form of an emotional content, and so can see little point in an art which rejects emotion as too human and not mechanical enough, and intellect as too exhausting. However, the 'easiness' of an object is one of the first conditions of its intrinsic value in this age. As I indicated, we are dealing with a race of overworked and distrait consumers. Since in art, as in everything else, they are more concerned with quantity than with intensity, each individual work must be striking and sensational, so as to be noticed at all, but at the same time easy and quick to consume, filleted and easy to digest so that nothing is left and there is plenty of room for the next pleasure. Both characteristics are to be found in the daily titbits which, as I have shown, the press serves up to the public in such large quantities. The social note is considered particularly effective and contemporary, but in reality it only produces scantiness and sensationalism. I quite agree that no material is impossible in itself, but however fine a social tendency is, it cannot compensate for a lack of artistic shaping.

This 'new objectivity' has led to another, equally doubtful venture in the specific field of music. I mean the musical guilds and societies with their amateur music and *Gebrauchsmusik*. This is a predominantly German movement which sees, quite

57

correctly, that today there is no society as a culture-medium for music, and so is trying to use the 'general public', as I call it, as a culture-medium instead. Its promoters are rightly trying to build up a new amateur-structure, but unfortunately they are doing it by trying to get down to the sunken level of present-day people. In other words, this is another attempt to combat the 'de-animation' of life on the ground of that very de-animation, and to compete with the 'convenience' of present-day objects. The error is that in the cultural field one does not have to compete in convenience—only in love, talent and effort. Imagine trying to write music so easy to play that even a distrait, overworked and unimaginative consumer feels inclined to buy!

Moreover, the serious amateurs of earlier times did not play the 'modern' music of the time; they were always a few decades behind. So if there are any amateurs, we need not doubt that in twenty or thirty years they will play the music of today, so long as it is 'vital', worthy and capable of constantly repeated efforts to get to know it. So the criterion of this vitality is not its 'easiness'. If every ignoramus could play the work of a contemporary writer because he had climbed down to the level of ignorance, this level would become a permanency, and the ignoramuses would take great care that nothing better should emerge, because they would already feel part of the whole thing, without having to make any mental effort.

Nothing has really been done about meeting the spirit of the age, in any of these ways. If earlier art epochs fitted the spirit of their ages, it was because age and spirit were not such opposites as they now are. I am not trying to advocate any one trend, or condemn any other, because really there are no trends. We know that the truly great works of every age are essentially alike, whatever historical 'movement' we neatly fit them into on the grounds of their equipment or some unimportant individual traits. Just as Expressionism, as a movement, perished because of the daubers who thought every ill-splashed canvas was an example of abstract painting, so Neue Sachlichkeit is dying of the support given by those who believe that every postcard is a work of art, that writing a drama consists merely of setting four out of five scenes in a brothel and filling them with the coarser swear-words. Fortunately a new movement will soon emerge and then we shall see that the good works of this period are still good even if nobody knows that they were once supposed to be Neue Sachlichkeit, or why.

It is humanity, directness, uniqueness, the originality of the experience that make a work of art, not the subject-matter, or the intention behind it, or the artist's attitude to an ephemeral public. 'Objectivity' is a process but not something to express, and to this extent every art, however Romantic, is 'objective' if it is good. For if so, it aims at expressing itself clearly, and this is the essential thing about every usable artistic method, whatever intellectual purpose it may be devoted to; in so far as any art attains this clarity it may be called 'objective'. Consequently I would like to mention the old Sachlichkeit, the good old Sachlichkeit of Sophocles and Goethe, Shakespeare and Novalis, Monteverdi and Schubert. And humanity, in the work of art, the fact that it centres on man and the things that always affect him—love, faith, hope, passion, intellect, grace—this humanity should only be new because we of today have to recapture it anew. The battle of the spirit cannot be settled on the level of the inanimate object. Nevertheless nobody needs to be afraid that he will have to abandon this age altogether (ridiculous thought—how could one?). For after all what is the 'age'? Us, all of us. And the people fighting against the age belong to it just as much as the others who think they comply with its demands better, but are really only giving up the ghost. Anyone who gives up the ghost is dead. But we want to live, and art is the highest expression of life. Consequently it is absolutely bound to assent to the 'ghost', the spirit, the mind, and if in this it is supported by everybody who does not want to be crushed by the 'business' of the period, nothing is really lost and no crisis can threaten the essence of art. It is a culture's business to ensure that art is not threatened from outside; we artists must take up some position in that culture—a very clear position, in fact—but we cannot steer it one way or the other.

THE FREEDOM OF THE HUMAN
SPIRIT

THE astonishing lesson taught by this interesting age of ours is that many things that used to be the great ambitions, to be ardently desired—things so real that beside them the fantasy world of art paled to a sad shadow fit only for the snappy businessman to smile at—splendid, glowing things like shares, bank accounts, factories, real estate, bills of exchange, as well as posts, salaries and wages—things like this have become as unreal, problematical, unsubstantial and chimerical as anything bred of the imagination. In itself this is, of course, very regrettable, but it has the unexpected advantage of suspending, or at least checking, the theoretical rivalry between intellectual life and the life of every day. Perhaps not everybody was fully aware that there was such a rivalry, but we felt it—usually it caused pain, always at least confusion—and owed many errors and false courses to it. It existed in two spheres—the purely practical and the intellectual. When I say 'purely practical' I do not mean that the artist was principally concerned to earn as much as a company director, but that art felt it had to compete with the huge resources of the entertainment industry in order to take and keep its position in the cultural life of today. Somebody has recently calculated that every evening in Vienna there are 75,000 seats available in public places of entertainment—theatres, concert-halls, cinemas, cabarets, cafés concert, in short everywhere where art is consumed like oxygen or beer. It emerged that this is about three times as many as before the war, an increase that is even greater when one bears in mind the smaller population and its considerably lower purchasing power. This enormous quantity, the possibility of supplying four per cent of the population every day with art or something like it, at any rate products calling for the same sphere of consciousness, must condition and alter the public mind, the intellectual stock of society, quite apart from the purely material effect, chiefly the dissipation of the money available for such purposes, which remains the same.

Hand in hand with this went a second, *intellectual* movement. Art has not only been pushed out of the public mind because of the enormous increase in art-type products, but also because, more and more, that mind has come to be filled with quite different sorts of things. I am thinking above all of the central importance of political and social problems in the last few years; they naturally tended to oust both the theory and the practice of art, unless art was prepared to absorb them within itself. Of course this does not mean that the artist was sitting at home, determined to practise art for art's sake at all costs, and is now wondering how he should mix his ingredients so as to be a match for talkies and political sensations. All these deliberations and intellectual movements take place in a much less primitive, compartmented way than I have to present them to make them comprehensible. The reality is that the artist automatically feels himself drawn into all these new and burning questions, that the struggle between artistic thoughts and aims and the social approach to problems, this inner rivalry, tries to work itself out within him.

First of all, let us take a look at the ideal of non-political art, which the liberal-conservatives yearn for with nostalgia today. I shall show that non-political or politically neutral, indifferent art is impossible, and that the ideal is merely a pallid illusion created by a desire for convenience rooted in mental laziness. Nevertheless there is a grain of justification in this aim, as in everything. It stems from a good instinct and a bad judgment. The good instinct is fed by the average cultured citizen's memory of the pure, incomparable effect of classical works and other works of the past that he has traditionally been brought up on. He thinks of poems by Goethe and Klopstock, perhaps also Uhland and Mörike, and laments the fact that apparently such pure, uncharged, independent, in short, beautiful, art is no longer being created. Admittedly he is confusing quality and independence. It is a great mistake to think that such apparently pure art was really unpolitical. What is more, our average cultured man is not unaware of these political links—he was taught about them in school. But they probably just remained dry bits of dead history to him; the political facts of the day struck him as merely a pathetic prop, because their matter did not *seem* pressing (in fact it was often much more so than is thought). So it never occurs to him that present-day writers are forced to take up a position just as the Classical and Romantic writers were, and that the political statements of past writers were just as full of contemporary allusions and apparently banal expressions as they have to be today. But while he can view, say, Goethe's allusions as paper evidence of a long-dead battle and enjoy them aesthetically, with the allusions of here and now he stubs his toe on the relevance that Goethe's allusions too had in their period. Quality is another question altogether: it is quite probable that the average art of today, considered purely from the point of view of its artistic value, its degree of talent, solid worth and assured craftsmanship, comes off considerably worse than that of a hundred and thirty years ago. But this is connected with the general decline and withering of substance, which no man can stop.

The wrong judgment I mentioned in connection with the ideal of non-political art concerns the content of what is recognised as art, and is in fact a question of confusing the programme of humanity with mere entertainment. It is only in the last few decades that art has become a way of relaxing after the day's work and that relaxation has become the aim of art. It is inconceivable that Beethoven's symphonies and quartets were considered by his contemporaries as welcome diversions to accompany the evening's digestion. At that time the average listener looked for more than distraction in his concerts and operas, and did not yet demand (as so many do today) 'something entertaining—there is enough sadness in real life, and at least in the evening one wants a little rest from it'.

Here we must clarify something that has been obscured by the development of the present period. The political and social spheres are not *a priori* identical; they are merely coming to overlap more and more because they are intertwined in so many ways. Politics are perhaps more concerned with the mental attitude of the human community; they are a product of the will of one or more of its members, and their aim is to construct a way of living which has a certain binding force. This mode of life is only indirectly connected with the social order, for it is not principally concerned with the externals of life—expenditure, consumption, industry—but with opinions, philosophies and outlooks. Under the pressure of economic problems and the growth of material needs, the social factor has gained the ascendancy, for the concerns of political thinking seem secondary, and what a mode of life can produce is subordinate to the goal of a social organisation that will do away with poverty. The demand for justice can no longer be banished from this technical-sociological line of thought, and this is a predominantly intellectual, ethical and hence political motif. The cry for justice is not exactly something new; it has probably been raised in every period, perhaps with even greater justification than today, for poverty and distress are not modern inventions, but things that existed, sometimes even more blatantly, in earlier times. But if I may put it in this way, those periods may have had the right state of mind for injustice, relying on the fact that the devil too had his place in world-economy. We have lost this hard but strong outlook; our social conscience has become more powerful because we no longer see a real relationship between suffering and achievement. What some people suffer does not correspond to what others achieve; we no longer believe in the economy of the whole community, in which the suffering of the one is the price of the greatness and glory of the other, because with regard to cultural achievement we suffer badly from inferiority complexes. But this, in its turn, is connected with the fact that we doubt the absolute value of this achievement and try to measure its real value in terms of its usefulness to society as a whole. We are not content to direct it to a recognised elite, but, dominated by the idea of public welfare, aim at the public at large. But at the moment this public needs purely material help, at a far lower level, and rightly declines cultural offerings it does not know what to do with. It is all the more risky to try to suit these cultural values to the capacity of the lowest level, whether one aims at the most primitive need for something undemanding with which to pass the time (the neatest solution, at any rate) or whether one makes it serve an ideology that uses people's dissatisfaction with present-day circumstances as a means towards party dominance. On the other hand it is difficult, if not impossible, to wrest the stimulus necessary for the creation of generally binding and notable works from the subjects which really, and rightly, concern the 'masses'. The world of culture, as we see again and again in history, has always been deeply, even if not flatly, tendentiously, connected with the religious world, and this, in turn, is the original and legitimate basis for the mode of life of a society, and consequently for its political aspirations. One might even throw out the suggestion that

65

when political orientation is determined by a total religious attitude, in the widest sense, an attitude that has absorbed the transcendental aspect of the human mind—when, as a result, the social element is subject to an automatic process that is secondary and stays in the background, this is the right social soil in which a true, worthwhile, generally applicable cultural crop, perceptible to everybody capable of it, can grow.

Even in the severest crisis the individual responsibility of a man remains fully intact, and every moment he has to choose between better and worse, higher and lower—in theological terms, between God and the Devil. I beg leave to consider this indestructible freedom of the human spirit as the highest good on this earth, and this evaluation as the true content of the religious attitude I mentioned; it is simultaneously the prerequisite of cultural achievement and the first achievement of the free, autonomous spirit, and so we come full circle. If this most essential contact is broken anywhere, the current is cut off and the desired achievement is bound to be absent. Man's wealth of happiness and sorrow, the fact that from time immemorial he has been lost in the impenetrable chaos of life on earth, his heroic and vain attempts to brighten the hopeless obscurity, the beauty and nobility of the human heart, the indestructible greatness of nature—these are the subjects we want to turn to, but the fanatical desire to preserve the value of these things is an eminently political emotion of the first order, and to that extent our art is political and cannot be otherwise.

What we consider the basis and prerequisite of human life, spiritual freedom in the widest sense, dignity and worth rooted in religion, is only graciously accorded to separate individuals; the mob, maddened by corruptors and forsaken by God, rage at them as though they were the arch-enemies of human society and will not rest until they have maliciously destroyed them. But is this a reason why we should give in and stop dreaming of freedom, of a wonderful state of affairs when life is of value in its own right and the moment being lived through is the only task and its own fulfilment? We cannot and do not want to. And so our song will always be aimed at the goal of nostalgia, even if it appears in the most varied disguises: the freedom of the human spirit and its undying power of choosing the good.

8

THE PROLONGED FUNERAL
BANQUET

RECENTLY there has been a spate of celebrities' centenaries such as can rarely have been experienced. The great are climbing down from Parnassus and pushing each other out of the way, like the shades before the ditch of sheep's blood in the Odyssey, in their impatience to get at the congratulations in time, for anybody who misses his anniversary this year is not very likely to be thought of later in the hubbub, and may well have to wait fifty or even a hundred years till his turn comes round again. Maybe that is not very long in terms of the eternity he has to endure, but it will be pretty annoying if in the meantime this period's lust for commemorations dies out. The living, for their part, race panting from one tomb to the next armed with calendars, excursion tickets and brief-cases full of commemorative speeches, and all take great pains to distinguish between the particular qualities of the shades they are conjuring up. Modest Raabe opened the season (and even he had to chase away the over-vivacious Mozart with a soft wing-beat); hard on his heels came mighty Goethe (but he has nothing to complain of—his turn comes round throughout the year, every now and then); his path was crossed by genial Haydn, and though we are concerned with him today, his much-loved spirit has already flown away to Orcus, ousted by Wilhelm Busch who has established his claim to attention in the meanwhile. And if I am not mistaken, a Richard Wagner Year is hovering in the distance, for after all even a fiftieth anniversary is not to be sneezed at.

In a period which indulges with such exclusive zeal in memories of the past it is difficult to establish the true significance of one of these figures, conjured up for a space and then dismissed, particularly when the work of the figure is so unfamiliar to the minds of the very general public involved in the celebrations. A few of Haydn's sonatas live on in memories of long-past piano lessons; those who date from the legendary period when chamber-music in the home was a relatively common practice know one or other of the string quartets; some vague memories of the church music linger mistily from childhood; one has a more or less vague notion of the oratorios and late symphonies —all of which does not amount to enough for a spontaneous act of national homage. Suddenly there is a hasty scrabbling in textbooks and compendiums, a consulting of reference books; it is discovered that he was one of the founders of the classical style of orchestral writing, although many object even to this and want to see other historical connections. For a week the music periodicals and supplements, feuilletons and illustrated papers are filled with a lot of semi-academic twaddle that makes the unprejudiced reader feel as he would if failed science students were to discuss the inventor of the steam engine after the coming of electrified rail traffic had long since made him a dead letter. Obviously this kind of publicity can say nothing valid about a man like Haydn, but just as the travel agents have to pretend that the world is open to all, even those who have not got the necessary permits to go to Boulogne, so it is the press's job to demonstrate that all our cultural heritage is common property, so as to flatter the reader's vanity and make him glad he has taken out a subscription. But quality is not really something that can be presented with enough persuasive power to have a widespread effect, and the qualities of the present, which have not been sufficiently tested quantitatively and in themselves are difficult to explain, are not a very favourable object with which to demonstrate everybody's supposed share in everything. Hence people have to fall back on the phenomena of the past, whose apparent indestructibility seems to show that their effect is greater in quantity. This state of affairs is in fact the reason why the products of the present-day are always rather disappointing material for a publicity system which has to impress a theoretically infinite quantity of consumers with quantitative ideas, which once again increases the cult of the past. Robert Musil summed it up excellently in his novel *Der Mann ohne Eigenschaften*: 'They were waiting for a man as solitary as genius and yet, at the same time, as generally comprehensible as a nightingale.' As to the great figures of the past, the solitariness of genius is assumed from the very fact that they were geniuses, which is deduced from their general comprehensibility (geniuses are always lonely, see numbers of anecdotes); but their general comprehensibility is hardly ever gone into—it is just automatically accepted because they are still being talked of one or two hundred years after their deaths.

Many of the articles have stressed, with much approval, that Haydn was a faithful servant of his master, patiently devoting a large part of his life to the service of Prince Esterhazy. I really cannot think that anyone who had such luck today would prove any less faithful. The good prince gave him food and shelter and allowed him to be as much of a solitary genius as anyone could desire. And when Haydn hit on the crazy notion of having four string instruments playing together alone he did not object and his guests had to see how they liked it. Apparently they did, or in the end the musician would have been dismissed and the nightingale engaged instead, but this proves nothing against a type of music which may perhaps be less acceptable to a totally different audience. If Haydn's music was generally comprehensible, to a certain extent, in its own sphere of influence, and he, as the stories go, was zealous in trying to

71

amuse his fellow men, that only proves something in the fellow-men's favour—that they were prepared to be amused by the worthiest and best. If that circle of men had developed and become more subtle as music has done since then, there would be no need to bemoan the discrepancy between genius and comprehensibility. If today the duly elected town councillors of Eisenstadt (let us assume they are the 'ideal' descendants of Prince Esterhazy and the company invited to his entertainments) had the task of appointing a musician to amuse their townspeople, the present-day Haydn would certainly fail ignominiously and they would pick a composing pedagogue with 'acceptable party membership', whose generally comprehensible military marches would soon make the nightingales in the town park sound hopelessly esoteric. For this reason the living are reduced to hungry fools whose tiresome work is to be laughed at or abused and the misunderstood shades of the dead are fed with the indigestible paper of commemorative speeches and writings while, at their inexhaustible table, people doze on, with paralysed brain, from one funeral banquet to the next.

9

WHAT SHOULD MUSIC CRITICISM DO?

HOWEVER you envisage music's function in the social system
—whether you see it as a means of diverting man's attention
from the fragility of that system or as something more or less
independent, autonomous, detached from real life—you cannot
help observing that its most radical, advanced emanations do
not correspond to an existing consumer demand: there is no
considerable body of listeners whose needs they are written to
answer. Nevertheless, works in the forefront of development
do exist, and no reasonable person can doubt their central importance to music itself, however small their market and functional value at first. The smaller the place these forms have in
listeners' awareness and the greater the inner difficulties they
put in the way of entering that awareness, the more important
become the things said about them and the judgments made on
them. As to these judgments, however, it must be remembered
—more than with any other manifestations—that a pure expression of taste can neither be just to them nor claim the slightest binding force for itself. The normative effect of taste-
judgments published by tacitly recognised authorities may
perhaps be legitimate in a compact society with tolerably unified cultural assumptions, starting from similar attitudes and
living in an age when no fundamental changes in the material
to be judged are taking place. Today such judgments are not
legitimate at all: first because the enormous change taking place
in music (and retrospectively calling into question much that
had been taken for granted) has removed the necessary basis

of a durable convention from any private taste-judgment and so robbed it of any lasting force; second, because the apparatus through which opinions are disseminated has made their originators, in relation to the mass of men who read them, into anonymous oracles, who cannot be checked personally and so are irresponsible.

All these factors together mean that an art-judgment which makes any claim to validity should steer clear of purely atmospheric mood-reports and concentrate on examining the music. This sort of examination is less popular and indeed fairly rare, because it demands considerable knowledge and gifts other than purely journalistic ones. But apart from that, it is less highly valued because people have become accustomed to consider the craft side of art as a self-evident and almost embarrassing adjunct to the daemon of creation itself. Instead they plunge into the interesting but nebulous depths of creation with a mistaken psychological curiosity which they first stimulate in the reader, because it is easier to satisfy, and then assume, with false regret, to be a necessity. The statement that something is 'well made' is now almost an insult and usually arouses the suspicion that the irrational, but hence all the more popular, 'spiritual' momentum has been beaten into second place by the workmanship. Now it has been sufficiently proved, not least by Ernst Kurth, that the psychological forces that naturally set the musical process in motion and keep it going, just as they do with all man's other intellectual activities, are completely bound up with the musical material itself and cannot be grasped or defined outside it: this, in fact, is the basis of the special quality of musical creation. Everything which can be said about music must necessarily be metaphorical, comparative and peripheral, unless of course it directly concerns its physical forms—the actual audible sounds or the visible notes printed on the page. It is obvious that such comparative presentations are the more problematical the less stable the nature of the thing compared, the musical material. So particularly at the present time, when basic changes are occurring in the organisation of musical material, music criticism ought to keep particularly strictly and carefully to these real manifestations of music and try harder than ever to derive its critical standards from the immanent laws within the material itself, instead of trying to derive them from inessential arbitrary systems of any kind.

The particular difficulty is that this very situation—all the bases of musical writing changing—makes it impossible to apply academic rules in a schematic way, as could perhaps be done with greater justification in other periods. More than ever before, it is a case of having to derive the laws of musical processes from the assumptions of each individual work—in other words of taking the law from the circumstances. The question is not whether a given traditional scheme is carried out or not, but whether an artistic organism is full of life, individuality, copious, deep presence, whether it is rich in ideas whose links and connections (or lack of them) must always be examined according to its own lights; the claims it makes should be compared with its real achievements and the task it sets itself with the way it carries it out; and the function of the parts in relation to the whole should be determined. In other words, what is wanted is analysis rather than value-judgments. Moreover the critic should most assiduously avoid suggesting that he has an arsenal of definitive footrules with whose aid he is able to measure everything worth knowing. For it has long been shown that there cannot be any such canons valid for all periods and phenomena, although this does not have to lead to a doctrine of aesthetic indifference. But the critic will be most certain of avoiding this sort of doctrine if he pins his judgments firmly on to the work's concrete factors; the conclusions that he draws from them will leave plenty of room to document his special personal choice of criteria. There will, doubtless, be lively, perhaps ineffectual discussions about the elements of a work which are quoted, but in so far as they concern things which are all present, and can be referred to, in the actual sound of the work, they should at least be more fruitful than merely expressing and disputing personal, indisputable opinions and preferences, which can only lead to a meaningless squabble.

After this it would be worth trying to establish the work's place in the development of the writer's work as well as in the continuous process of stylistic transformation. Here one should avoid, above all, the useless and misleading quest, so dear to the so-called 'fundamental critics', after purely external similarities; instead one should look for some sort of historico-philosophical interpretation. An analytical criticism of music along these lines could be thought of as an 'extension of reproduction' and as such would be more important and valuable to work which is venturing into the unknown than mere empty praise or blame that does not hit any real target because it starts out on a false premise.

It is not only because most of the people doing newspaper criticism have neither the gifts nor the training for anything but 'taking sides' about art in a way that cannot be checked objectively that newspaper criticism usually exhausts itself in the sort of praise and blame outlined above. It is also due to the social function of criticism, which is forced on it by the character of the machine through which it is published. Art has become a commodity whose sale depends on the exchange value of the products, and this value depends on their intrinsic value, which is determined largely, as a result of a curious pretence, by criticism. It is a pretence because both the public who are to pay for the commodity and the performers who sell it are thoroughly convinced that the critical judgment is not binding. This conviction goes so far that it is sometimes even used as a weapon by critics who have been caught out in a mistake due to carelessness or corruption; they defend themselves by saying that in any case nobody takes them seriously. Let us say no more about the curious professional ethics this attitude reveals—the fact nevertheless remains that the public does not rely even on the most prominent authorities, while the performers, although they are equally well aware of their actual powerlessness towards both the work and the public, shy at badly reviewed works, merely out of fear of a 'bad press' (they suddenly ascribe power to it when it concerns themselves).

With the best will in the world the scattered handful of highly gifted critics can do nothing about the fact that critical opinion has been devalued by bringing the publicity machine into the business—not because doubtful morality is forced on them (this is rare) but because the character of the daily paper automatically makes the readers turn first towards the propaganda value of any opinion expressed in it.

Admittedly the form of music criticism advocated here— extending the reproduction in an analytical way—would need a good deal of display and space and so would perhaps be difficult to fit into the framework of daily journalism. But music criticism could only gain in authority if it was not necessary for it to cover every trifling daily event that wants its performance-price marked up, and if it could work in a more dignified way instead of playing the role of an obscure and anonymous Star Chamber sandwiched between sensations and advertisements in the hurly-burly of the daily press.

10

NATIONALITY AND ART

A WAVE of growing national self-awareness is sweeping over the world. Even the economic troubles which ought, in all reason, to be an argument for international solidarity (theoretically supposed to have reached an advanced state already) serve only to strengthen the tendencies towards encystation and self-seclusion—tendencies that are put forward as cures for the self-same ill that caused them, or at least exacerbated them. The various nations' essays in autarchy naturally have a far deeper and more radical effect in the sphere of cultural affairs than in any other, because they are much less hampered by objective hindrances than are other things—so that it seems as though incursions into this area could be made without catastrophic material consequences—and because cultural, especially artistic, achievements, being pure products of independent imagination, appear to each nation instinctively to be the flower, the most perfect expression of its nature. Obviously a heightened national self-awareness will try with special passion to gain mastery of this easily accessible, largely visible and particularly sensitive sphere of activity.

Now obviously it could only be gratifying to the artist to be recognised by his own nation as a radiator of its spiritual energies. In any case he is one quite automatically, even if the nation does not recognise him as such. The idea that this fact needs special verification and confirmation is the first error of the new nationalistic concepts. It grows out of the second and greater error, which is that they do not choose to view *everything* that the nations produce—after centuries of reciprocal relations with the widest variety of races and peoples—as their own characteristic production, but think they can specify the 'national' forms of expression on the basis of a collection of material characteristics chosen from outside and pronounced to be characteristic. But the historical picture of a nation's cultural life is not defined by such externals, but by individual achievements of genius which are created within it: the soil in which they grow is—with certain reservations, of course—something to be accepted from the beginning that cannot be prevented from showing itself, however unconsciously, and neither needs nor is susceptible of explicit confirmation in the work itself. The fact that, say, Goethe wrote out of a background of a German type, and Balzac out of one of a French type is an incontrovertible reality. But it would be a complete reversal of the truth if one were to explain the essential power of these geniuses by showing a certain correspondance between their achievements and a 'national personality' defined *a priori*. On the contrary: it is their autonomous greatness which first gives concrete substance to the concept of a national mentality extending over a shorter or longer stretch of history and shapes the cultural habitus of a nation. The greatness of a national personality is in no way determined by nature, but is created by the greatness of the things achieved within it. Consequently this greatness cannot be determined by the one dependent on it, but only on a basis of the autonomous laws of art; it is to be compared only with its own kind, to be measured by its share of the eternal values, not the transitory ones that seem to fit the present situation of a 'national personality' impossible to define objectively; and it is to be recognised by asking how far the work rises above the material prerequisites (which include national factors) into the sphere of truth. For the outstanding can only be recognised by its share in the general.

Quite wrongly, this approach is often stigmatised with the derogatory catchword 'internationalism'. A recent important pronouncement on the subject told us that 'the Greeks did not build in an international way but in a Greek way' or something of the sort. No doubt: but the universal validity and enduring beauty (enduring so that we too can perceive it) of Greek buildings certainly does not derive from a slavish attachment to the folkloristic details of a local tradition that we no longer understand, because it was dependent on premises no longer current. What still matters is the intellectual force with which individual Greek geniuses outgrew the natural factors and created forms whose value, enduring through time and space, first established the greatness of Greece. Greatness has never taken up a vaguely cosmopolitan attitude, its aim has never been to suit the average man's taste (unlike, for example, popular music, which is a trade commodity and so aims to suit as many situations as possible). The truth is that it is the works that stand out by their individuality and originality, that result from a unique, unrepeatable first-hand effort, which achieve the real general validity that makes other nations want to learn about them. And it is the cliché-ful 'average' works that never make anything but a local effect. The more average the works, the more similar their habitus, and the less apparent their individual—and hence also their national—origins. It is the mediocrities who shout loudest for a 'national' art, which they conceive mainly as a stereotyped use of arbitrarily chosen, folkloristic and purely external formulas. This kind of aim is doomed to failure, because it is in fact the unusual work, the work that cannot be neatly fitted into any code of rules but is a legitimate descendant, in a purely spiritual way, of the unusual work of the past, which achieves universal validity and the ability to cover the national image with the desired glory.

One fact is wilfully ignored by most nationalists and also,

oddly enough, overlooked in the critics' theories, although it seems of decisive importance: this is the circumstance that the Occident, consciously or unconsciously, whether it likes it or not, lives in a state of Christianity. Nationalism, if consistent, is forced to reject the essence of the Christian concept, universalism. And yet it is only this very concept that offers the Western world the nation-linking attitude that makes it possible to create and perceive values on an international scale—indeed, looking backward, establishes the debt we owe to the classical world for our whole cultural life. This being so, it should no longer be at all possible to persist in the materialistic naturalism that seeks to enclose men within predetermined, self-contained groups in which, being subject to the instinctive, inborn, impulsive-driven conditions of their physical nature, they are for ever trapped. Whether you define these groups as classes or races, the effect is the same—it is only replacing one materialism with another. To say that the philosophy of a national or racial community, precipitating itself in moral values, is dependent on its national character and valid for that only, is in fact to proclaim an ethical relativism diametrically opposed to Christian thought. This is the attitude that really threatens the 'decline of the West', in whatever geographical position and under whatever auspices it may arise. It is very doubtful whether a secularised world, which thinks it can ignore metaphysical matters in general and reduces them in practice to a dull respectability or propriety can cope with this danger. Perhaps the way out of it will present itself most plainly in the field of art, which is the hardest one to handle and the one which reacts most sensitively. It can only find it if it acknowledges that this late period, highly differentiated as it is, can no longer use a real or stylised ur-language as a means of expression, and that art is only entitled to the name in so far as it can prove its share in the transcendental.

11

KARL KRAUS AND ARNOLD
SCHOENBERG

Two Austrian men whose nature and work show strange points of contact, despite the enormous difference between their characters and fields of creation, have completed their sixth decade this year: Karl Kraus and Arnold Schoenberg. It is not because they are neighbours in time and place that one thinks of their two names together, but because of the streak of inexorability and intransigence that they share and which has led both into a strange position of public solitude, although this is quite a different solitude in each case. The main feature of Kraus' incomparable work is plainly a certain conservatism: he perceives a God-given harmony of mind and nature which he realises in language, the first home of man, and sees localised historically in past literary ages crystallising round the mighty figure of this or that poetic genius—and he is anxious to protect this harmony from the onslaught of ruin and decay, disguised as technical progress. On the other hand, Schoenberg is usually venerated or execrated as a revolutionary destroyer of the current codes of law. And yet in his own way he too may be called a conservative spirit, for what is thought of as his 'avant-garde' quality is only the most complete, the truest possible fulfilment of the law, never an irresponsible, frivolous break with it. He resembles Karl Kraus in that he, too, wages his war against 'the existing order' on its own ground, and, by insisting on a complete and utter faithfulness to the prevailing code, aims at taking it *ad absurdum*, showing how it contradicts the higher laws of absolute morality. However, Schoenberg's war is not primarily a moral one but an aesthetic one, and this shows what completely separates these two basically similar minds: it stems from the different values of the two fields in which they work in relation to a generally valid moral scale.

Music is the art furthest from life and is completely without 'subject-matter', a purely elemental phenomenon, so that it does not express extra-musical thoughts but *is* the sum of purely musical ones. Consequently in its inner development it is subject only to its own autonomous laws, and the radicalism in the conservative demand for complete fulfilment of the law can only have a moral effect indirectly when this radicalism leads to new music's having difficulty in fulfilling its natural function —being heard by listeners—because of the mental laziness of the first audiences. One can only see a moral achievement in the self-sacrificing way a composer sticks to a course he has seen to be necessary, in his absolutely uncompromising consistence, which defies all obstacles. Language, on the other hand, being the vehicle of thought, is actually part of the moral world; it makes possible, indeed *demands*, a moral achievement from the writer who has recognised the immorality of a situation caused by wickedness and stupidity—and this moral statement is made directly, without having to pass through the filter of an aesthetic revolution which arouses opposition. Now in so far as Schoenberg's work is primarily carried out in the aesthetic language, which is largely separated from the moral one, he always has an opportunity to make a purely practical effect *via* half-understanding, snobbish convention and sensational shock, but his judgments cannot be absolutely binding on anybody but those of his colleagues who have enough courage and discernment to follow his line; so that many believe they can somehow bye-pass him and legitimately create music without coming to terms with him. But one can see that experiencing opposition to his artistic course, which made Schoenberg's moral force ever stronger and more manifest, gradually became the stuff of his work. At first it occasioned his polemical literary writings, but in the *libretti* he wrote for himself it increasingly became the substratum of his artistic activity and the field of application for his aesthetic achievements. So the moral and aesthetic spheres worked together more and more, while the moral intransigence, originally deriving from the need to stick to his aesthetic guns, now became their justification. In this way Schoenberg approaches Kraus' creative law, according to which the two spheres are completely and inseparably identical from the beginning, although this cannot be true for Schoenberg, since he is a musician. Hence Schoenberg's moral achievement, originally due to the consistence of his artistic attitude, primarily leads only to an aesthetic judgment which is not binding in the final moral analysis.

The artistic perfection of Kraus' work specially authorises him to be a spokesman, and being tied to language it belongs entirely to the moral sphere and leads to a moral judgment which is absolutely binding. Consequently he has not got the opportunities for practical effectiveness which result from misunderstanding, indulgence and love of sensation and always occur in the aesthetic field. But on the other hand, for anyone on whom his words have told, there is no escape, no way of cloaking a detour with a threadbare theory that still clings to life. He can only follow in all humility or vegetate in the sad knowledge of his own qualms of conscience and depravity, as numerous people have already done. Under his rebuke the seductive line of least resistance is impossible to take, while it always seems promising in music, just because of music's moral indifference. But for this reason the musicians who think they understand Karl Kraus will not be afraid to take the decision Schoenberg forces on them, even if it deprives them of some practical effect in this world.

It is remarkable and significant that these two men both emerged out of the Austrian decadence in 1874—both of them destined to cause a truly salutary disturbance of vital importance to European culture.

12

ON THE STATUS OF WESTERN
MUSIC

'WESTERN music is distinguished from that of nearly all other cultural areas by having developed an extraordinarily rich and constant autonomous branch subject to intensive transformation.' This fact has often been stated though perhaps not always correctly appreciated; above all, its causes and consequences have not been examined. There are tendencies towards autonomous music—that is, music that exists for itself alone and is not *used* for anything—in other cultures; but it is only in the West that the main accent is on autonomous, unapplied music, that the changes which affect the development of the whole art take place in the sphere of autonomous music, and that autonomous music is indisputably representative of music as a whole. In no other culture has music succeeded in producing independent forms as rich, both internally and externally, as our chamber music and symphonic music, and nowhere else has it succeeded in giving such autonomous forms the central intellectual significance which they fundamentally have for us, in principle. Beethoven, Brahms and Mahler are valid symbols of their ages —even to the non-musician they are obvious representatives of the most important intellectual resources of their day—yet they only wrote 'abstract' music which is not co-ordinated with any practical purpose.

In other cultures music as an art stands mainly in a position of strictly determined dependency on religion. But secular music too—songs, dances, etc., which are more freely written, perhaps improvised—hardly exists apart from its application, and in any event does not grow into larger independent forms. The artistic centre of gravity is undoubtedly the music bound up with religious ritual. In this connection one of the important signs is that music is not put at the service of religious practice as a finished article; from the very beginning, in its very origins, it is rooted in religion. Not for nothing is it usually a deity who has given music and its rules to man, according to legend. Music's inclusion in the religious sphere is not only something going back to its origins, but a sort of prophylactic, for music was considered to exert enormous, uncanny influence on the humours of those exposed to it. It was a dangerous kind of magic which had to be kept under the surveillance of religious officials. In fact this basic attitude is an undercurrent that runs right through the typically western mentality from Plato to Tolstoy.

These two factors have hindered not only its independence, but its historical progress. Music's ritual character petrified it; the fact that its rules had been transmitted to man by a deity meant that changing them was sacrilege, for carrying them out was a direct act of worship. There can be no doubt that these attitudes—less clear, and of course less naïvely credulous, still persist as atavistic residues in the common rejection of anything new in art. Above all, the additional overlay of heated fanaticism and wild anger with which artistic progress is so often obstinately rejected, is more understandable if one puts it down not only to laziness and an aversion to unusual sounds, but to a kind of superstitious fear of offending against charmed, magic rules. This idea is supported by the fact that tradition is so often called 'a law of nature', while more advanced music is castigated, with an almost comic lack of proportion, as a kind of act of violence aiming at the overthrow of world-order.

This sort of idea is atavistic because it overlooks the fact that western music has long escaped from the magical taboo, simply because Christianity became the religion of the West. Unlike the primitive religions Christianity is not a tribal faith, but a universal message of salvation. Not being tied to any one chosen people, it offers grace to all, including the 'barbarians', of course with the reservation that they must 'debarbarise' themselves and become citizens of that higher Roman Empire which is the spiritual, Christian version of the ancient, adventitious empire of the real Rome. As the rituals of the first religions were tribal, their sacred rigidity and unalterability were a kind of self-preservation, a way of ensuring the nation's existence; they were symbols, fetishes of a deification of the special qualities of the tribe. Greek antiquity had already prepared the way for intellectual values to be freed from the magical influence of the tribe; through the universal message of the gospel, Christianity finally made that liberation secure and established intellectual and cultural values as of universal importance. It was Christianity which first made the concept of 'mankind' into something concrete, real. Christianity first made it possible to relate intellectual achievements to mankind as a whole. It is due to Christianity, too, that a hierarchy of these achievements emerged, wherein the top ones are those in which the relationship to mankind as a whole, to 'man' as a type, emerges most clearly and deliberately; while all the others that relate to any kind of limited section rank lower, however highly their individual quality may be esteemed. There is no doubt that every sort of universality, in the sense of super-national relations, derives from Christianity and would be unthinkable without it, because it represents the first practical spiritual community embracing all men. The nearest thing to it is the similarly supernational concept of the Roman Empire, but this is far behind it, as any secular, organisational concept must be behind the concept of a religious community rooted in the super-natural.

Again, it was through Christianity that music first became a universal expressive form with an intellectual content, because it was no longer part of a tribal ritual established by a national religion. It grew from a magical phenomenon, forming vital elements in order to fix them in myth, into a rational phenomenon freely expressing thoughts and feelings. Thus the art-music of the West is primarily Christian music, that is, a music which, conditioned by the Christianity of its listeners, expresses a spiritual element common to them all; indeed Christianity is the only common factor which determines the community —all others, such as nationality or language, are of lesser importance. It is important today more than ever, to keep in mind not only the greatness of this conception, but its origin, and to have as clear and concrete a picture of it as possible.

Only since the universality of Christianity has existed has the concept 'exotic' had any real meaning. Something is exotic when it is only related to one more or less limited section of total humanity; but it could only be recognised as such after there had come into being expressive forms which corresponded to *total* humanity. In the pre-Christian world, where cultural life was divided into self-contained monads, everything was more or less exotic in relation to everything else. In other words, the term had no real meaning. Only in the Christian world can one see a continuous stream of cultural achievements related to the whole, and everything outside that mainstream appears exotic, with all the charms of originality, picturesqueness, local colour, and all the weaknesses of the insignificant, trivial, provincial and commercial. Of course, as it flows through history, this mainstream is fed by many local streams and many of its sections are coloured, to a greater or lesser degree, by the national tributaries flowing into them. But a nation can only make the mainstream run through its territory as long as it has the will and the power (through its geniuses) of raising its national individuality above the level of the exotic and drawing general validity of expression from it. It never works if the nation complacently stresses the exotic quality of its special character and sees keeping to that special character as its ideal. As we know, the mainstream of generally valid European music crosses Dutch territory in its upper course and then later runs through Germany, Italy and France alternately. It flowed through these cultural areas whenever their inhabitants had the strength to raise their individuality to the level where it was expressive of all Europe, and the insight to subordinate the folkloristic, exotic element to the human and general.

The first manifestation of Christian music was liturgical, just as the music of other cultures was religious, and its raw material was oriental, like the geographical origins of Christianity itself. But as Christianity was not a tribal religion of limited validity, this oriental material took on a very different meaning as it spread over the Occident. Developing into Gregorian chant, it became one of the bases of Western music. The music historians claim that it is the foundation of the 'linear', 'horizontal', melodic conception of music, the point at which were established the principles of serialisation, the melodic 'basic figure', as the centre of reference of musical passages, the variation of fixed melodic elements. This was supplemented by a 'Nordic' element—the principle of symmetry, demonstrated in rhythmically articulated periodic structures, one balancing another. The history of western music, which cannot be examined more closely here, presents itself as a continuously changing correlation of these two groups of principles, the accent and point of view being constantly altered and the combinations constantly varied.

To take the broad lines of this history, without going into the many intermediate and mixed forms, it may be said that at the beginning the linear approach dominates. This is the period

91

of the Middle Ages which led to the Golden Age of Netherlandish polyphony. The 'Nordic' material, in the form of periodically articulated folk-tunes, was by no means neglected, but the formal principle on which the foundation of medieval music was laid did not come from this 'Nordic' side; it tended, rather, to be subordinated to the opposite tendencies, as an 'exotic' breed.

At the same time this is the period when the centre of gravity of Western music is in the sphere of church music. The fact that there was also a large quantity of highly developed secular music which simply was not recorded, so that we know little about it, does not make the above any less true. For surely it is no accident that this secular music was not written down, however many practical reasons may also have existed. The decisive reasons were undoubtedly internal ones and the fact that this music was not committed to paper is direct evidence that it was not of the same cultural significance as contemporary church music. All crucial cultural achievements automatically ensure their own preservation in paper form, force themselves to be written down in unequivocal symbols that time can tamper with as little as possible. The degree of care taken to fix a work's text unambiguously and make sure it is inviolable increases automatically in proportion to its significance. Secondary work has no need to last for ever and is content with an approximate record of its improvisatory form, or does without it altogether, recognising its own ephemeral character. External reasons—the fact that the composers have not learned to write, or that preservation is not thought necessary, etc.—are always only a consequence and confirmation of the internal reasons. Christian, and hence Western, music had not developed an autonomous branch at this period, and so its crucial development took place in the sphere of church music.

A fundamental change occurred in the Renaissance. After

freeing music from its ethnic commitments, Christianity now freed it from its connection with religious content, as it now also freed the other areas of culture. The supremacy of secular music dates from this period; it is only now that the autonomous music that we described as the unique prerogative of the West begins to develop. It should not be forgotten that even this music, in so far as it is a universal form of expression (and this is its essence and the unalterable basis of its significance) is inconceivable without the assumptions of Christianity. But only now did it construct the autonomous, unapplied forms which became the valid symbols of the cultural attitude of whole ages and hence characteristic of the West as a whole.

This process was, remarkably enough, linked with the fact that the 'Nordic' elements gained a good deal of ground. 'Vertical', harmonic thinking, division according to symmetrically arranged formal elements now won the day. The result was the disintegration of polyphony; it was replaced, very flatly and elementally, by the monody of the *stilo rappresentativo*, of opera, in which the homophony looks externally like a recreation of the oriental style, the primitive state of European music; but through its indissoluble link with the chord-columns erected on the counterpart of the *basso continuo* there emerges a completely new picture, no less unequivocally European than the polyphony of the Middle Ages. Of course the term 'Nordic' is to be taken with a grain of salt. It is meant to indicate those elements native to Europe as a whole which Christian music found as it grew up in the West. They were of course of a younger and more primitive type than the oriental ones and consequently their dominance was linked with a definite simplification of European music in post-medieval times. The new music made up in effectiveness and direct comprehensibility what it lost in density and richness of structure. This is why medieval music has been almost entirely expelled from the modern consciousness and is only appreciated historically, but it is also why a new development in the opposite direction, which has begun in this century, has had such extraordinary difficulty in making its way. By its very nature this direction cannot, like the monody of the High Renaissance, enter with the superb gesture of destroying past shackles, liberating music from old-fashioned pedantry and making it a form of expression for all humanity. The movement I am thinking of enriches music internally by giving it completely new possibilities for construction, but externally it seems to limit its comprehensibility and direct effectiveness, because its connection with Europe's 'natural resources' is not so direct as in the golden ages of post-medieval music; it tends rather to look back to the medieval relationship in which the musical natural product was less the source than the object of artistic work.

The direct connection between modern music and the European natural heritage is also the cause of musical nationalism, which became more and more marked in the nineteenth century, parallel with a corresponding process in other spheres of life. The universality of Western music, preserved despite its secularisation, reached its peak in the cry of the last movement of the Choral Symphony—*Seid umschlungen, Millionen*! From then onwards this accumulated light was broken down more and more into the various national colours of its spectrum. European music 'exoticised' itself, though the first steps in this direction tried to continue what seemed to be the tradition of 'world music'—as, for example, Czech and Russian music looked first to Wagner and then to Debussy. Objectively, the best work was done by men who were radical about their nationalism and did not try to follow 'world music', such as Mussorgsky and Janacek. But even Wagner and Debussy are not universal as Beethoven was, but national phenomena, even if not so strikingly 'exotic' as those of the European fringe-nations, because they cultivated a much older and less virgin territory.

It is certainly no accident that the idea and substance of a universal western music lived on in Austria, whose last great period was that of the Wiener Klassiker, and that it was there that it was completely renewed, with all the necessary characteristics, in the twentieth century. Not for nothing did Brahms practise and preserve Beethoven's methods of composition in Vienna; *via* Brahms Schoenberg linked himself, first indirectly then directly, with Beethoven, when he tried to give a new syntax to the new musical language that rose out of the ruins of the old one. Just as Austria is the last resting place of the old universality and, let us hope, the germ-cell of a new one, so it is the cradle of a new concept of total-Western music through a rebirth of the linear, melodic, polyphonic qualities that characterised the first epoch of European music. The other types cannot and should not be excluded, any more than in that earlier period, but the confrontation of the two components, which is the story of European music and without any doubt the cause of its wealth of splendid, inexhaustible variety, is being carried on from a new standpoint. One can feel the characteristic natural material being penetrated by this cultural universality in many features of Béla Bartók's work; it is clearer here than on our own heavily built-up area, because the clash between it and the unused material still available is more prominent. Is our modern music's obvious appeal to universality and polyphony a symptom showing that secularisation is being supplanted? It is impossible to answer this just with brief allusions to one omen or another. When such a process occurs it can only do so over long periods and probably unknown to the very people carrying it out. But it is indisputable that musicians are now aspiring towards a new high order, in keeping with the true dignity of Western music, and that is as far as we can go within the limits of this essay.

13

IS OPERA STILL POSSIBLE TODAY?

STRICTLY speaking this question has been asked in every period since the puzzling and contradictory affair which is opera has existed. There is no need even to consult the huge mass of theoretical writings on the problem of opera; the numerous opera-parodies, which are almost as old an institution as opera itself and faithfully attend all its various manifestations, are proof enough. Many of the parodies outgrew the original target they had aimed for, and themselves created new styles, thereby giving new life to the very object of their satire—one need only think of the *Beggars' Opera* in early times, later Offenbach and Nestroy, and in the present era the collaborations of Brecht and Weill and many features of Milhaud, Hindemith and others. One of the essential points about these parodies, I think, is that their darts are not only aimed at the particular contemporary manifestation or style of opera which inspired them; they nearly always attack the essentially operatic features of opera in general. It is not only the values of Handelian opera, by then felt to be stilted, that the *Beggars Opera* was attempting to reveal as vapid, and not only Meyerbeer's high-flown attitudes that Offenbach attacked in his *Barbe Bleu*, but 'opera' as such—and moreover always on the basis of the rational argument that it is absurd for people to 'sing' while doing things which are obviously part of normal life. The question of whether opera is 'still' possible nearly always implies another question—is it possible at the pitch of rationality then reached to swallow the 'nonsensical' essence of opera with equanimity and credulity. Objections of this more aesthetic sort are immediately supplemented by the doubt as to whether it is permissible from an ethical point of view to continue this nonsense, when it obviously contains a fair amount of falsification. Carrying out such an exacting type of nonsense often contrasts with the questionable reality of life itself and this leads to sociological considerations that in the end take the question of opera's possibility out of the purely intellectual, cultural sphere and into a completely practical and material one.

The reason why the nature of opera is called into question again and again in this way doubtless has to do with the fact that opera is an artificial product, in the most literal sense. Whatever crises the theatre may go through nobody directly questions its right to exist, nobody doubts that the theatre is a relatively 'constant' activity of the human race—the proof being that its origins are lost in the mists of legend and myth. Opera, on the other hand, at least the form of musical drama we call by that name, is not only a very young form but has clearly visible and even rather suspect origins: it was invented, in a rather cold way, by literary men who were quite remote from any current of musical feeling. Everyone has heard of the papers of the Florentine *camerata* of enthusiastically humanistic aristocrats who used many of their meetings to create as faithful as possible a reconstruction of Attic tragedy and ended up by finding that their experiment had produced opera.

It is obvious that however one may imagine Greek drama was performed, opera does not bear the slightest resemblance to it, not even the opera that was the result of those early scholarly experiments, let alone opera as it later grew and developed. Yet, although this fact was fairly self-evident and became ever more so as research into antiquity progressed, the questionable link with classical drama remained, for some strange reason, a decisive factor in the development of opera. All the 'reformers' of opera, from Monteverdi through Gluck to Wagner, made their ideas revolve round this imagined revival of Greek drama, and often tried to justify the boldness of their innovations by adducing their similarity to the spirit and practice of classical Greek dramaturgy. Wagner, who of course was no longer so ingenuous as to believe that his music-drama resembled Greek tragedy in any technical particular whatever, tried to claim that his 'total work of art' at least had the same sociological functions in relation to the wished-for German nation that Hellenic festivals had in relation to the community feeling of the Greek nation. This is a rare phenomenon—a purely paper fiction gaining a very genuine power over the reality of an area of life and culture merely through the force of values and attitudes it had conjured up itself.

The so-called 'reforms' which revolutionise the development of opera from time to time are always concerned with giving the intellectual content of the language and drama a new, more crucial position. All the innovators agree in seeing operatic singing as a kind of heightened speech—from Monteverdi who tried to re-create a 'Pyrrhic' style he had dreamed of by using the enormously dramatic and bold means of rapid note-repetition, to Richard Wagner, who went to great trouble to demonstrate how the musical conception grew out of the dramatic and linguistic one. These reforms always seem necessary, because opera, when left more to itself, shows a tendency to become an exhibition of vocal qualities and singing achievements. These fulfil a sensual need of the public's, and explain why the 'reforms' were and are so passionately fought against at first: they rob opera, for a time at least, of its pleasurable, sensual quality.

This is, in fact, the point from which today's criticism of the opera-phenomenon principally starts. The idea is roughly this: it is a pure fiction that opera can be given a significance higher than sensual pleasure by shifting the accent to the language and drama; this is merely a sort of rationalised superstructure which serves the 'reformers' as an excuse for creating new and hitherto unexploited forms of vocal exhibition. The proof of this is supposed to be that the daring and hotly disputed innovations of their day, once they have sufficiently taken root in the consciousness of opera and the public, end by revealing their function as pleasure givers, and hence are then defended against further innovations. Wagner, the argument runs, is not prized and admired for the new quality of his total art-work, as he intended, for the way the music heightens and underlines the significance of his dramatic conceptions; he is valued because, despite all these speculative achievements, the public has learnt to track down the purely operatic side of his work, the side that appeals to the sensual instincts; moreover all his intellectual apparatus only had the result of extending the pleasure-potentialities in the sphere of opera. From this the conclusion is drawn that opera only has life in it in so far as it can satisfy the need for pleasure. And it is not possible for opera to exist in the present day, it is objected, because as regards society in general it cannot compete with the cheaper and more direct pleasure-givers which can satisfy the relevant needs of large social classes much better. What is more, it is not even a desirable thing for these classes to be offered pleasure-givers of this or any other kind, for they distract their attention from much more important general matters.

However much justice there is in this reasoning, it does not entirely get to the heart of the problem, in that it accepts the category 'pleasure' undialectically. It may be true that the first impulse to listen to opera is a desire for the pleasant sensual impressions it induces. But as the desire to produce these impressions is not the only motive for creating opera, the additional—or rather original—values are felt in 'consuming' the pleasure and through the pleasure itself, so that it too takes on completely changing virtues. These special modifications of pleasure have been studied by Bert Brecht in particular, and his *Mahagonny* is the significant result of these studies, not only having pleasure as a subject but also presenting what it has to say about it in the form of opera, which is recognised as a particularly 'pleasurable' form. Nevertheless it must be admitted that the conclusions Brecht draws from his doctrine are not perhaps entirely unequivocal; they are certainly not the only possible conclusions. For it should be noted that although at first the 'pleasure-seekers' reject anything unusual as a bar to pleasure, they really crave it, unwittingly, because in the end they grow tired of the pleasure they cling to so stubbornly. Because novelty is rejected in this way, the innovators always produce polemics against the purely pleasurable function of opera, and to this extent it is true that their theories can be viewed as the framework which supports their innovations. But the really important thing is just the inescapable urge of the truly creative nature to express something new, and viewed from this immanent angle the question of opera's continued feasibility depends purely on whether there are sufficient creative gifts with the need and ability to express something new through the medium of opera. Compared with this, the problem of whether this new element is able to exercise the pleasure-giving functions, or whether and when it will itself become a mere pleasure-giver is entirely unimportant.

To assess correctly the inner justification and feasibility of opera today—and only this can give a worthwhile answer to our question—one needs to examine how the new element manifest in today's opera has altered opera's substance. And here it may be said that this new element eminently justifies its existence in the face of all sceptical opposition, in that it accepts the contradictions with which opera is reproached and tries to make them dialectically productive. First of all, there are all the tendencies towards destroying the illusion of opera as a self-contained form, the tendencies which underline the 'non-sense' of sung words. In contrast to Wagner, who aimed to make the medium of music-drama so tight and self-contained that it could exist autonomously side by side with—or best of all, instead of—spoken drama, without the question of its principles of existence ever arising at all, they accept that there is a wide gulf between sung and spoken drama and that the one is not an organic, gradual heightening of the other, but an artificial world quite opposite to it.

This destruction of the pretence probably stems from Romantic and Baroque stylistic principles, but in the form in which Cocteau and Claudel have introduced it into the world of opera it means something completely new. Claudel, in particular, has originated the idea of dividing the stage into various levels on which things happening at different times can be played simultaneously, often intertwined with one another. To this trend belongs Brecht's demonstrative-didactic style, in which the action is interrupted by observations, discussions and explanations, so that the pretence of a self-contained formal whole is destroyed. It is interesting that after being in at the birth of opera, literary men have also provided important impulses at various later turning-points of its history.

These impulses would of course remain infertile—indeed they would never occur at all—if new possibilities on the musical side did not tempt creators to approach the dramatic element in a new way. If it had not been for the musical upheaval that made itself felt in the most decisive way at the turn of the century, the writers just mentioned would hardly have thought of applying new ideas to the dramatic aspect of opera. The very fact that in music fundamental changes emerged from the development begun by Schoenberg made the musical element as

102

such take the limelight—a move that had been heralded by Debussy's attitude, which was, of course, considerably removed from that of Wagner. Busoni's attempts at neoclassicism and the reintroduction of old, clearly demarcated forms into opera music are further heralds and symptoms of the new attitude. For the first time in operatic history, perhaps, a movement intent on saving clear musical form from being flooded by the stream of realistic drama is not a reactionary symptom; for once people are trying to safeguard the musical side just because the changes made within music are radical. This neo-classicism only takes on a reactionary character when and where it confines itself to reconstructing archaic forms and tries to take no account of the new musical achievements.

Unlike the reactionaries who, in the name of 'pure musicality', have always opposed the 'reformers' starting out from the dramatic side, the new, musically orientated current within opera does not aim to increase its sensual pleasure in the customary sense. In fact the new musical language has just the opposite character; its radical quality tends rather to heighten the feeling of alienation. With the further advance of 'atonality' —that is, the new, radical musical language—the emphatic use of old forms has disappeared too; at first they had served as clear signs of a resistance to the anarchic arbitrariness of dramatic 'truth' (even in *Wozzeck* by Alban Berg these old forms, though camouflaged, play an important if already rather outmoded part). This movement too rests on the ideology of a higher reality, but unlike the ideologies of the early 'reforms' of opera, which always thought reality could be attained by laying more emphasis on dramatic realism, on 'expression' (actually, of course, this only created more stylising factors, for opera is a stylised drama by definition)—unlike these, then, the new movement tries to get reality not by perfecting the illusion, but by doing away with it altogether.

103

Taking the ending of pretences as the basic intention of a new operatic style makes opera a particularly pregnant expression of the antagonistic outlook of the present age and at the same time makes it the very opposite of present-day political tendencies, which, whether of the right or of the left, go in for concealing antitheses and simulating a united, coherent world—and do not scruple to use force to do so, which in itself is the most blatant symptom of internal paradox.

The rôle of the opera chorus shows very clearly just how earlier opera reflected the outlook of its age and what changes have taken place in this respect. In the early days of opera the chorus was the element that, at least in form, came closest to the dream of reviving Greek tragedy, but also the element that linked the new musical form with the medieval style it had cast off. The new, revolutionary element of opera was the solo singing, moving along on light harmonic props and following the accents of speech; the chorus (as in Monteverdi's *Orfeo*, for example) remained separate, chiefly presenting its reflections on the dramatic fates of the individual characters in the polyphonic style of medieval choral writing, in which it was not the single voice but the vocal part (descant, tenor, etc.) that was given an autonomy skilfully fitted into the organisation of the whole. Later opera simplified this structure more and more, and extended the laws of harmonically based monodic writing to the chorus parts as well, at the same time bringing the chorus into the dramatic action. The chorus no longer stood outside the drama, but now that it was inside it it dwindled to a mere accessory. It was neither—as a group reflecting on the action— an 'ideal' antithesis to the individual actor, nor—as a differentiated 'crowd'—a real antithesis to him; it was simply a multiplication of individuals round the single individual, usually banished to the beginnings and ends of acts where it demonstrated the completeness and amplitude of the operatic world hidden behind the curtain and was meant to indicate that its fictional existence continued before the curtain rose and after it was lowered. Any branch of the 'lower orders'—townsfolk, soldiers, huntsmen, sailors, monks or whatever—could be the accepted subsoil out of which later the individual actions grew; and its existence was supposed to be made credible by its harmonically solid and formally complete singing.

At the stage of musical development reached by Wagner such a simplified and musically amorphous type of choral writing could no longer be accepted, and Wagner's most radical conceptions, the *Ring* and *Tristan*, draw the logical conclusion and eliminate the chorus entirely, apart from a very few rudiments. The beginning of Act III of *Tristan* when the curtain rises on the hero's solo lament, is the sharpest possible contrast to the traditional act-openings, when the curtain usually rises on a sonorous swarm of crowd, which later disgorges the soloist. But even here the fiction of the continuity of the composer's invented world is preserved. Only modern opera deliberately rejects prologues and epilogues; sometimes the curtain is even raised before the music begins, in silence, to stress that we are to witness a deliberately organised performance and not to be abducted on the magic carpet of music for a few hours in an unreal world that exists in its own right.

The current development of musical style is giving the chorus back a polyphonically structured autonomy, and so once again it can, as a spectator and commentator, form a contrast with the action, or, if it takes part in the action, contrast with the individual as an element governed by its own laws.

In view of the present state of the world one may well wonder whether opera is still feasible in another way, for opera's central concern is with individuals (in fact this was the original reason why it was invented) whereas the historical movements of this period are dictated, deliberately or not, by

105

the masses and their fate. There is no room here to discuss how far this theory is valid; but it may be observed that wherever the masses, as such, become a factor in artistic expression, forms emerge which must be considered reactionary, if looked at from an objectively artistic point of view. It is completely immaterial whether the ideology behind the writing is reactionary in the political sense—trying, that is, to keep the masses in a subject position—or whether it calls itself revolutionary because it is trying to create a new state of affairs. The best proof of this is that wherever either of these ideologies, apparently diametrically opposed, is in force, modern art is outlawed. From now on art's 'progress', which can be recognised objectively, will be in the direction of the individual, and hence it will want the art-form of opera and make it feasible. As this is quite the opposite way to that in which the age as such is progressing (I cannot go further into this at the moment) it is undoubtedly the cause of all the changes and peculiarities of the new opera under discussion.

The musician consulted about such problems has no choice but to start from the subject he knows about, the special laws applying to music. Consequently the facts that have emerged from the modern development of the musical language have to keep on being emphasised. And it is this very transformation of the musical language that has drawn attention to the special inner technical laws of the musical material, after Romanticism (particularly in its later phase) had principally stressed symbolical qualities of music which could be appreciated in an extra-musical way. Hanslick's well-known description of music as 'form moving in sound' is taken for granted to a certain extent, but the reactionary formalism that derives from it has been conquered. Consequently playing off Verdi against Wagner, a pursuit so often encountered in the new opera movement, is the sign of a false, superficial and purely literary approach.

Neither composer can be claimed as an unambiguous reactionary or an unambiguous progressive. Wagner's doctrine of the total work of art is now revealed as an auxiliary construction to support his internal musical innovations, while Verdi's apparent traditionalism contains so many forward-looking forces that in the end, from a historical point of view, they both achieve much the same result.

What distinguishes the present transformation of the musical language is its emphasis on the autonomy of the musical element, the fact that it establishes the validity of music as a means of communicating ideas. In this its function is equated with ordinary verbal language. but it differs from it in that musical thought does not exist apart from its manifestation in sound and so cannot be expressed or described in words. In a sense, then, music seems to be the pre-logical original form of language, subject to the same laws but carried out in a completely different and autarchically self-contained medium. So in modern opera music is not merely a means of heightening, ennobling verbal language—it is not there to make the words more eloquent, so to speak; it is deliberately contrasted with the words, placed behind the words, making them transparent so that you can see their second inner significance. As an illustration let me quote just one passage from Alban Berg's *Lulu*, where Alwa offers the exhausted Lulu a liqueur, after she has been released from prison and has returned to Dr Schön's house. He utters only one word—'Benedictine'—but this everyday, even banal utterance is made so much a part of the composition of Lulu's indescribably beautiful entrance passage that it is virtually a peak of ecstasy. The music does not achieve this by 'heightening' the words but by opening an abyss of meaning and countermeaning behind them: here the Benedictine is not just a liqueur such as you offer a guest, but a true love-potion.

Modern music is striving for new forms suited to its own

language-structure and in opera it meets up with the literary tendencies I have mentioned—the tendencies to break up self-contained theatrical form and destroy the illusion of a self-contained world. The fact that this open-work dramaturgical technique is very obviously influenced by films does not make it any the less true that it is in rapport with the most subtle peculiarities of atonal music-development; on the contrary it proves it, for these dialectical forces, which today are disrupting the concept of self-contained, static systems in every field, are very evident in the way film sequences are cut and combined. All this ties up with the quickening of tempo characteristic of modern opera. In opera the dramatic tempo is always determined by the proportions according to which the musical form unrolls in time. In the early days of opera, with Monteverdi, form is generally very terse, although this is often concealed by numerous da capos, verse repeats and similar devices. But at the same time there is the comparatively 'formless' (actually shaped with all the more skill) form of the free monologue, which was to assume such gigantic, extended dimensions in Wagner, as was demanded by a tonal music now dissolving into chromaticism. The move to atonality converted this great quantity into a new quality: musical form—that is, the mode of presenting musical thought in a time-dimension—once again becomes terse, often microscopic, compressed into epigrammatic form, confined to sharply profiled gestures. The reaction this has on the form of music-drama is obvious: the opera scene works in detail like a slow-motion camera, because singing naturally extends the words, but over larger stretches it speeds up processes to a certain extent, for in modern musical tendencies there is no room for anything static, symmetrical or repetitious. This is not the place to go into the details of the development of atonal music, which was created mainly by the twelve-tone technique; it must suffice to mention that the forms that emerge as particularly logical from this development correspond, to a great extent, to the efforts to open up the self-contained world of drama. I will just name two of the attempts that have been made to produce new results along these lines: *Christophe Colomb* by Claudel and Milhaud, and my own work *Karl V.* The great changes in musical and dramatic attitudes have made it possible for present-day opera to include in its orbit important and intellectually difficult matter, without merely picking out some picturesque trait or other to represent it, as Romantic opera had thought to be the only possibility. Now opera can work out its real central significance. From the purely technical angle, the quick tempo and scenic conciseness make it possible to cover much more extensive complexes of material; but above all, since the new operatic style aims at antithetical tension, allusions which break up or crack the apparently consistent whole, it can probe into the deeper intellectual strata of the theme treated.

The practical side of the Is-opera-still-possible question still remains to be discussed, now that the question of its inner feasibility has been answered with a wholehearted 'yes'. Here one is bound to start from the fact that music faces more difficulties than any other art in getting across, uninterruptedly, to the public mind—and not only because of the internal reasons connected with its type of stylistic development, but above all because the 'standard repertoire' has thoroughly jammed up this would-be 'continuous' process in the last century or so. Before that, almost nothing but 'new' operas were performed: that is, a new opera would generally be written for each occasion which demanded the special luxury of an opera performance, and only a certain few works were repeated. It was only in the nineteenth century, when the majority of opera-lovers were no longer members of the aristocracy but, increasingly, middle-class people, that the urge for familiar, older works began to grow, that the tried and trusted was demanded again and again, and new operas came to be more and more the exception. Finally, in this century, complete stagnation has set in and the repertoire practically never takes in a new work. The circle of works that come round again and again is, to all intents and purposes, a closed circle, and when (with increasing rarity) something new *is* let in, it is shot out again immediately afterwards almost as speedily as in the seventeenth or eighteenth centuries, but for the opposite reason—not because something even newer and less familiar is wanted, but because people are anxious to get back to the old, well-known favourites as quickly as possible. This, the normal situation, was only masked for a few years by the fact that German opera-houses, with their enormous resources, seemed ready and able to try new things on a large scale—but the standard repertoire was not enlarged there either. Now that this little outburst is over, the facts as I have stated them are plainly visible.

To forecast the future of the standard opera repertoire is neither possible nor necessary within the context of this essay. It is enough to say that one would not give much for the chances of an organism that never takes in fresh nourishment (and if it does make the attempt for once, almost always makes a mess of it). The natural tendency of the commercial opera houses is to do any new work with the minimum expenditure of time and effort, for since experience has proved that in any case such works do not serve to enrich the repertoire, they can only reasonably be considered an interruption to the standard repertoire work as such. Moreover the new operas are much more difficult to perform, technically; this is unavoidable because of the way style has developed. It follows automatically that the really important new operas will find less and less place in the normal opera repertoire and, increasingly, special occasions for presenting them will have to be sought out. In fact

110

this tendency can already be observed when a normal commercial opera house sets about doing an unusual work and tries to give this performance the character of a special gala occasion. This tendency towards a certain 'exclusiveness' is not at all a bad thing for the important new opera production. Of course 'festivals' of this sort have nothing in common with Wagner's vision of a representative, almost religious, national sacrament, but are, rather, concentrated demonstrations of artistic ability and achievement in the form of works whose intellectual and material content justify this kind of special effort. The fact that under this system there are far fewer opportunities for performance than with the old repertory arrangements must be borne as the necessary price of the development I have described.

At the same time new opera might conceivably find a home for its potentialities in the externally much less demanding framework of a kind of touring theatre, if it could develop suitable types which, without giving up the present-day attitude to musical expression, would use such simple external equipment that they would be within the powers of a touring company. For touring companies, like special productions, have the opportunity for plenty of preparation, in numerous rehearsals (this is indispensable and justifies itself because the opera is repeated over and over again in various places). Up to now, however, not much positive action has been taken along these lines.

Nevertheless, all these practical problems are of secondary importance, however much they affect the very existence of all involved. The essential question is whether opera as such still has an inner life-force, and I think the above considerations lead us to a decided 'yes'. It should not be forgotten that opera is an unusually young genre, and in the three hundred years of its short history has certainly not yet evolved a definitive form for itself. So although the general picture may give the opposite

111

impression, it can hardly be said that our age is just not operatic and hence hardly 'oper-able' (by comparison with, say the baroque age, all of whose emanations seem to have something operatic about them); the form of baroque opera was suited to the general style of the age, but it was not *the* opera form par excellence and quite a different form will suit our completely different style of living. Of course it is conceivable that at some time opera will die out—this would have to happen if individual singing was no longer appreciated as a medium of dramatic expression. Musical style has changed in such a way that this possibility has to be considered, particularly when one observes how performers caught in the old tradition find it extremely hard to adjust to the new demands. But as to that, the force of ideas always wins against material opposition, and just as Wagner's apparently 'unsingable' writing found convincing interpreters, so will the new operatic style, though with far greater difficulty because it does not emanate so clearly from a single extraordinary personality and is not merely a still unrecognisable fulfilment of the age, but its deliberate opposite. But there is no doubt whatever that, for the present at least, there are more possibilities still open to opera than it has yet explored.

14

ALBAN BERG'S *LULU*

THERE is one reliable, objective starting-point from which to examine Berg's *Lulu*—the relationship between his libretto and Wedekind's original (the two dramas *Erdgeist* and *Die Büchse der Pandora*). The main aim of Alban Berg's adaptation is to reduce the length without sacrificing dramatic motifs or whole scenes. The four acts of *Erdgeist* form the first act (in three scenes) of Berg's opera and the first scene of the second act, and the three acts of *Die Büchse* form the second scene of the second act and the third act, divided into two scenes. Thus the break between Wedekind's two plays now comes in the middle of the second act of the opera. Into it Berg has fitted the story of Lulu's conviction and release from prison; he has solved the almost insuperable difficulty of presenting this complicated story in musical-dramatic form by showing it as a silent film accompanied by music. This central point in time is also the dramatic centre of the work: the turning-point in the heroine's destiny. Until then she has been active, inciting men to ruin through the instincts she unleashes in them; now she is passive, and the guilt of middle-class morality weighing down on her makes her the victim of the exploitation-instincts lurking round her, and drives her to ruin.

The ruthless cuts Berg had to make were naturally not only quantitative; they also lead to a certain internal simplification of Wedekind's conception which, although concise, is full of ramifications. But the purpose of this simplification is to stick more exclusively to the tragedy that nature itself has imposed on Lulu, the original Woman. Of course this is the central concern in Wedekind's plays too, and of course Berg has not cut out the other sides of the drama—the satirical and polemical ones—altogether, but the way in which he shifts the emphasis is very indicative of the special structure of his character.

Berg's nature was markedly polemical and satirical—a specifically Viennese characteristic if one considers how many of Vienna's best brains were of this type. Nevertheless he had too clearly defined a picture of the demands of the musical theatre to let his satirical gifts have much influence on that side of his work. He generally used them privately, when collaborating on polemical publications. Nevertheless the operatic ideal he was aiming at was also, in a sense, characterised by Viennese intellectuality. The basis of the ideal was to become completely absorbed in the mystery of Woman, which is seen as something insoluble, and to keep circling round this complex of thoughts and feelings, which are felt to be the centre of all human experience. This line of thought and emotion can, of course, be traced back beyond Goethe's Faust and many elements of early Romanticism, but it reaches a culmination in a certain development of post-Wagnerian German opera. It seems as though the great boiling-point of emotion, the hitherto unknown affective intensity that Wagner's music drama made as frightening as it was exciting, became an indispensable part of opera in general, and people felt themselves forced to plunge into the tragic passions because the source of continuous ecstasies seemed to gush out from them. This applies both to the rather flagellantic ardour of Pfitzner's *Der Arme Heinrich* and Richard Strauss's more cosily decorative gallery of female colossi. But above all it is true of the exotic phantasmagorias of Franz Schreker (now largely forgotten) whose often excessive naïveté can stop one realising just how directly they reflected the mind of that generation—just because of that naïveté. Another factor which tends

114

to be overlooked is the great local influence of the Viennese scholar Otto Weininger, whose tragic suicide put a very desirable halo of demony around his learned contribution to the problem of 'Eternal Woman'*. But the most obviously connected world is perhaps Arthur Schnitzler's—this strange world given up to its erotic impulses no less helplessly than sensually, and gilded over with the dreamy light of lush autumn afternoons, sinking consciously, pleasurably, into the ruin that the apparently irresistible urge of its nature is preparing for it. And it should be remembered, too, that this was the short but intensive heyday of the Jugendstil, with its water-, reed- and marsh-ornamentation which it had taken from the earliest days of matriarchal culture, a comparable eruption of all the erotic, elemental side of life.

All these factors play a much more important role in Berg's life and work than is usually thought, and they are so bound up with the experience of that generation that we may well ask what would really touch us closely in Alban Berg if these factors were as exclusive of all else as they are in Franz Schreker, a man only a few years older. Without trying to persuade ourselves that our level of development is 'higher' in any respect whatever, we are bound to see that the demands we make on the musical theatre are on quite a different side—the intellectual side. We are much more concerned with the intellectually antithetical aspect of drama, shown in the collision of spiritual forces and pointed in the forms of intellectual dialectic. But in this, Berg is one of us; for his concern with the erotic problems of that generation is always linked with an eminently constructive imagination which enables him both to make contact with the intellectual outlook of the young generation and to penetrate his material with the new spirit in a unique way.

The two men who influenced Berg most in this matter are

* das Ewig-Weibliche—the eternal feminine principle.

Arnold Schoenberg and Karl Kraus. To Kraus the Ewig-Weibliche is the mysterious centre of man's nature—but it is also the purest expression of the original divine principle, undisguised essence, the primal order before the fall, the real likeness of God. This automatically puts the male world of wanting and doing into a dialectical relationship with this Ur-nature; it becomes the central principle of the Fall, of ambiguous thought and intellectualism, which must be paid for with punishment and repentance. The repentance produces the creative principle of male organisation, demonstrated most clearly in the act of artistic construction. This rather brutally simplified account may sound too Romantic—but on the whole it contains the nub of what concerns us here. For Alban Berg was always saved from sinking mindlessly into the intoxicating cult of the Ewig-Weibliche by his love of strict construction. Small wonder that with this overall disposition he turned to Wedekind, whom Karl Kraus was always defending on the grounds of a similar disposition. Wedekind's inexorable style cuts through the whole territory of passion and emotionality in his material with enormously potent sharpness and yet bleak sobriety. Only a shallow taste could see inadequacy or cynicism in what is really the conquest of the cheaper passion by the higher one of the mind, the imaginary pre-logical state of nature being defeated, or rather overtaken, by the great discipline of construction. This is the significance of Kraus' and Wedekind's compositions in words, and it is equally the significance of Alban Berg's musical conception. And it was Kraus' first production of *Die Büchse der Pandora* in Vienna in 1905 which gave Berg the decisive impulse that made him write *Lulu* almost twenty-five years later.

With Kraus it was the sacred mystery of language in which the paradisical element, transcending guilt and innocence, lived on, to manifest itself in language's crystal-clear rules, expressed in its knife-keen dialectic; with Berg it was preserved in the strictness of the musical law formed by a man of similar mentality, Arnold Schoenberg. When the nightingale, speaking for the bird-world in Kraus' poem, says 'you have the law, we have the world', it voices an opposition of the most profound kind between the pre-logical sphere which is the real domain of the female nature, and the sphere of law which is thoroughly dominated, with inexorable logic, by language and the norms of art. But the more faithfully, exactly and self-forgetfully the law is carried out, the more likelihood there is that the mind which has become self-aware will be attracted by that other region of unreasoned happiness that comes before all awareness. Berg's work always lives up to this duality, which constitutes its tragic element and also its significance: and it is more manifest in *Lulu* than in any other of his works.

There is an obvious parallel between Don Giovanni and Lulu; in fact Berg pointed it out himself. It goes deeper than the immediately apparent similarity—the insatiable erotic appetite of the two characters. As Annette Kolb has rightly pointed out in her book on Mozart, Don Giovanni only grows from a rake into a tragic hero because Donna Anna is forced to love him although he is her father's murderer. Lulu, on the other hand, only changes from a pleasure-seeking doll into the fury of erotic destiny because she is condemned to love the brutal, cowardly Philistine, Dr Schön. It is not because she remains cold amid all the consuming fires she kindles but because in this one case she herself burns hopelessly, that the paradise of love she seems made to create becomes a desert of horror and destruction. It is the merit of Berg's adaptation that this aspect stands out with great clarity. Again, the inner, as it were moral, balance of the piece is strikingly brought out by the idea of having the three men who complete Lulu's humiliation and ruin in the wretched London attic at the end, played by the actors who were also the three men ruined by her in the first part of the tragedy. What these two basic figures of erotic mythology have in common is the despair that Kierkegaard has conjured up in his magnificent study on *Don Giovanni*. Of course there is this difference, that Don Giovanni's despair, which dogs him like a bad demon, drives him to tempt the divine kingdom of the dead, and it is this which causes his downfall, not his actual erotic extravagance—whereas the effect of Lulu's despair is immanent in her. The one thing she never wanted to sell she finally has to hand over all the time, for a lower and lower price, because once, just once, it did not achieve the enormous price her destiny forced her to put on it. This demonstrates not only the difference between male and female tragedy, but also the decline of the motif as western culture has developed into a world of commerce and trading. Don Giovanni is pure myth; Lulu is a myth which has become aware of itself and turned into cultural and social criticism. In its remorseless blatancy the idea of the bourgeois man who did not want beauty as a gift forcing it to sell itself to his own kind is an attribute of a rationalised and secularised mythology.

This essential difference is exactly expressed by the musical characterisation of the two types. Of course I am not going to compare Berg with Mozart, but rather the historical situations of music in which the two men had to create and which made one of them choose one type of material and the other another type. When Mozart appeared on the scene, the principle of tonality had not been at all disrupted. The paternal world dominated by the father–idea was still thoroughly valid and the norm against which Don Giovanni offended was represented by the norm of major/minor tonality to which the tragic hero himself belongs. How different from the picture of disintegration for which the tragedy of the despairing woman strikes the composer as an adequate expression. The very in-

118

tellectual consistency which saved Alban Berg from sinking into the naïve, unreflecting swamp of the Jugendstil's matriarchalism, the ruthlessly intellectual musical thought stemming from Schoenberg, caused the destruction of tonality, the break-up of the firm musical foundations which had supported the masculine type of artistic order.

A detailed musical analysis of *Lulu* would be too specialised for this essay, and so I shall confine myself to this general interpretation of the work's musical habitus. Compared with *Wozzeck*, the 'programme' of *Lulu* has become stricter in the technical sense, as Berg composed *Lulu* on a single twelve-tone row, after the later development of Schoenberg's doctrine. Nevertheless the overall sonic impression of *Lulu* is sweeter, gentler, softer, more attractive than that of *Wozzeck*. This is an expression of the dualism in Berg which I mentioned at the beginning. He did not use the step forwards which he took by accepting the twelve-tone technique as a basis for a similar step forward into new intellectual territory, but rather to legitimise the fact that he was lingering in the familiar philosophy of an earlier generation. For him the new technique was a way of preserving the lost country of this sweet, decaying beauty for an age that had left it behind. The country presents itself as a kind of illusion (which is why it is devilish, like all paradises) and the illusion is constructed as Adorno has very exactly described it: it is treated as though it were a new truth. Consequently Berg's later work has a touch of noble sentimentality which should be noted without the slightest criticism. Berg used the new musical construction, which had destroyed and scattered the old type, to hymn the beauty of its decayed predecessor. In fact the new one served him as a way of expressing enormous sadness that a new one should be necessary. There can be no doubt that this is why Berg is the only one of Schoenberg's intimates to have a real success during his lifetime. *Lulu*

119

is the tragedy of beauty—that is the plainest, simplest explanation—but the beauty undergoes tragedy because it manifests itself as an inseparable attribute of decay. The lost country of tonality, of the beauty of that masculine-ordered world, is reconstructed in *Lulu* with the means of a new, unknown order which was both the cause and the result of its decay. And so it is exemplified in the indescribably lovely and yet doomed picture of the woman who destroys that beauty, yet nevertheless represents it in all its glory.

Berg's idea of making Lulu a coloratura soprano indicates how in the erotic sphere Ur-nature and intellect meet on the ground of refinement: here what is birdlike, part of nature before its 'animation', is identical with the late artificial element that reveals a cold numbness in the curve of passion. The same idea is at the back of the characteristic timbre of *Lulu's* orchestrations, a select mixture of vibraphone and saxophone: the sweet, even sentimental tone of the saxophone's exaggerated vox humana is frozen by the cold bell-tone of the electric vibraphone, the hot throbbing of emotion is changed into the cool shiver of refinement.

The way Lulu's song is composed shows how the intellectual element has both a calming and a stimulating effect on the passion. Lulu's dialectically opposed aphorisms, completely unrealistic in their subtlety—'You knew why you married me just as well as I knew why I married you', or 'If you are sacrificing the evening of your days to me you had all my youth in exchange'—have a melodic form (reversal) that exactly matches their contradictory content. This principle is most triumphant in the film that comes in the middle of the work: the scene of Lulu's release from prison is accompanied by a strict reversal of the row-sequence that accompanied her committal; the events correspond down to the smallest detail of the properties and from a certain point onwards the music too is retrograde down to the last note.

But the parallels with *Wozzeck* that Berg has deliberately introduced into *Lulu* lead further than just into the intellectual sphere and make the work a component part of the great personal confession that his oeuvre represents. The fourth-motif with which *Lulu* begins, looks back to essential melodic patterns in *Wozzeck*. In fact they can be traced right back in his work to the period of the songs to postcard-texts by Peter Altenberg— those wild, powerful early works which have been completely forgotten since the tremendous tumult that their partial first performance in Vienna caused in 1912. An even more remarkable instance is provided by the three chords that close the three acts of *Lulu*. Each time one part is lowered by a semitone so that the four-note chord that ends the whole opera is the characteristic chord accompanying the decisive moments of Marie's part in *Wozzeck*. In both cases it is preceded by the horrifying action with the knife, the man's murder. In *Wozzeck* it is the individually characterised man himself, brought to the point of despair by the doom of nature, who grasps the murder weapon as the *ultima ratio*, which can bring him revenge for the unspeakable sorrow he has suffered. In *Lulu* it is the dreadful anonymous spectre of the sex-murderer which tries, in this frightful way, to re-establish the justice which has apparently been violated by Ur-nature itself. The nameless murderer's horrible deed is the male gesture in itself, but it is identical with the innocent gesture of the child who cuts open a doll to see what is inside. Beauty is murdered after it has plunged everything round it into dreadful ruin, because somebody wants to rip out of it the secret of why its effect must be so terrible. The executioner walks away unconcerned, but the secret remains a secret.

'Walk in, walk in, ladies and gentlemen,' roars the lion-tamer. The curtain goes up and Alwa asks: 'May I come in?'

And his father repeats the invitation: 'Just come in without any ceremony.' Neither of them suspects that he is going to fall into the power of the man-eating mystery. At the very moment when Dr Schön hopes to escape, he has to fall, with his eyes open, into the flower-covered abyss of lust; and in just the same way Alwa still sings the dithyrambic hymn to beauty although his eyes have been opened by all the catastrophes he has lived through.

We may be sure that a man who lived so much in cipher-symbolism of all kinds as Berg did must have been deeply impressed by the similarity between the sounds of Alwa and Alban. And with that heroic hymn of defiance, this artist, bewitched by the sweet sphynx, so demonstrated his conscious attitude to the mystery that the most horrible destruction will sound the final chord on that wonderfully played harp, in that death-cry whose perfect construction as twelve-tone music and as an integral part of the new order will proclaim the end of that highly praised, execrable beauty as nothing else could.

15

NOTES ON KAFKA'S COLLECTED WORKS

FRANZ KAFKA'S long short story *Der Hungerkünstler* ends with the sad death of the artist, who has been forgotten by everyone: nobody takes any notice of his artistic starvation in the circus cage, and it is only when they need it for something else that they find the dying artist. He is buried, 'but a young panther was put in the cage . . . he lacked for nothing. The keepers brought him the food he liked without pausing for reflection . . . joie de vivre radiated from his mouth with such heat that it was not easy for the spectators to withstand it . . .' This is the same motif as at the end of *Metamorphosis*, the same feeling of release from a nightmare, a release shattering in its heartless unconcern. There the family, freed from a son who also had perished in animal solitude, take an electric train out into the country and savour the primitive animal enjoyment of life after weeks of horror. But the motif of a ruthlessly healthy panther is surprisingly reminiscent of another passage in Kafka: in the *Observations on Sin, Sorrow, Hope, and the True Way* no. 20 runs: 'Leopards break into the temple and drink the sacrificial vessels dry; it happens again and again; in the end it can be calculated in advance and becomes part of the ceremony.' Here the two spheres are directly contrasted—the free, unrestrained nature of the beasts of prey and the organised ceremonial trying to draw that nature into itself. This second, human sphere attracted Kafka as much as it horrified him; it is the world of bureaucracy within which most of his epic works take place (*The Castle, The Trial* and many of the short stories). The office becomes so enormous and all-powerful in Kafka's conception that in the end the whole world appears to be a giant office, more particularly on account of its mysterious inscrutability, for the nature of the office, too, is mystery: the supposedly clever but completely impenetrable system of intertwined operations that has to be humbly accepted by the 'party' just as it is, like a distant solar system whose workings cannot be influenced. For a few years Kafka worked in the Workers' Accident Insurance Company in Prague, and so was actually a part of this bureaucracy that he raised to a mythical level. A passage from a letter to a friend is very characteristic of his attitude towards this sphere: 'I have the passport; the new passport-issue reform is wonderful; the interpreter, fumbling after, cannot keep up with the increase bureaucracy is capable of, necessary, unavoidable increase, stemming from the source of human nature, which source, in my opinion, bureaucracy is nearer to than any social arrangement. It is too boring to go into further details—too boring for you, that is, who have not been happy standing for two hours in the crowd on an office's steps, at getting a new insight into the business; who have not trembled, when receiving the passport, and when answering an unimportant question—trembled with real, deep respect (with ordinary fear, too, but certainly with deep respect).'

This is exactly the way of experiencing which activates the figures Kafka creates, the feeling that the world regiment is led by a huge, illimitable bureaucracy whose secret is that it is practised in dull, dusty grey offices by subordinate figures who themselves have no idea of the meaning of what they do within the framework of the whole, while it is completely impossible to have even a notion of this framework, or of a central position at all—the thought alone is a punishable offence and threatens the offender with dangerous consequences. This basic attitude is exemplified not only in the long novels but also in many of the shorter stories, particularly those that deal with the building of the Chinese Wall and with China in general.

Attempts have often been made to explain the special quality of Kafka's thinking in terms of Judaism. I cannot judge the importance of this kind of interpretation, but even if it is completely correct it seems to me too specialised; nor, I feel, does it do justice to the scope of Kafka's work. It should not be forgotten that as a writer Kafka belonged to the Bohemian province of German writing that has become known, once and for all, as a branch of Austrian literature, since the illustrious example of Adalbert Stifter. Admittedly many ironic traits in Kafka's style, his often-quoted love of paradoxes, can be explained by a Jewish attitude of mind, but his link with the German classical tradition carried on by the Austrians, is manifest not only in the extraordinarily disciplined use of language characteristic of all Kafka's writings (except perhaps a rather 'expressionistically' scintillating prentice work, *Die Beschreibung eines Kampfes*, but in his belief in the majestic rule of law, eternally circling round us—a belief he often expresses in a bizarre and ironic form. The ability to see the religious concept of the law embodied in a secular bureaucratic complex is undoubtedly based on the theocratic strain which is still inherent, most unambiguously, in the Austrian conception of the state, and can be traced to its direct descent from the 'Holy' Roman Empire. The similarity between this and the Chinese concept of the empire is sufficiently well known to explain why Kafka so often gave his stories a Chinese setting.

The law carries with it the destruction of anything that comes to belong to it, even if there is a special distinction in this, as there is in the deepest fulfilment of the law. This doom approaches stealthily, quite secretly, and often remains unrecognised, even when it has already arrived. Usually it is merely a question of unremarkable little changes that would perhaps have been stopped at the beginning if they had been appreciated then. But that is just why they are not recognised and it is they that introduce enormous evil which can never be undone, by gradually drawing the dazed person, step by step, into this calm, majestic machinery. There can be little doubt that this idea of being sucked in was inspired by the experience of illness, which attacks a man in exactly the same way: in Kafka's writings it appears in a wide variety of forms. For example, it is not hard to identify the unknown 'animal' in his last story (*Der Bau*)— an animal whose uncannily approaching whistling and hissing disturbs the peace of the large, cleverly planned subterranean building and threatens to destroy its inhabitants—with the tuberculosis which so early tortured Kafka to death. But in this there is also fulfilment, and so on the one hand the law is out-side, where the 'animal' lives and the pitilessly healthy panthers leap, and on the other it is inside, where the regularity of the building reigns and the eternal, indestructible office is para-mount—or rather it is both inside and outside in insoluble, paradoxical conflict. This is an essential medium of Kafka's style —by no means a specifically Jewish attribute, but an attribute of Christian dialectic—one has only to think of Kierkegaard, in whom Kafka was very interested. This sentence from the *Meditations* grows, in the most genuine way, out of the style: 'Idleness is the beginning of all vices, the crown of all virtues'— what a surprising and true conclusion, drawn from the stylistic necessity alone.

The unusual vividness of Kafka's description, effected with a simplicity and terseness reminiscent of Stifter, helps to make his paradoxes so lucid. It is this imperturbable objective tranquillity that produces the horror so peculiarly characteristic of Kafka's stories; this passage from his diary is characteristic too: '. . . I think of the nights at whose end I was roused from a deep sleep and awoke feeling as though I had been imprisoned in a walnut.

A terrible vision last night—a blind child, apparently the daughter of my aunt from Leitmeritz, who in any case has no daughter . . . This blind or weak-eyed child had both eyes covered with spectacles; the left one was milky grey, round and prominent behind the lens, which was quite a distance in front of it; the other one receded and was covered by a flush-fitting lens. For this lens to be optically correct the usual sidepiece over the ear had to be replaced by a lever whose head could only be attached to the cheekbone, so that a piece of wire ran down from this lens to the cheek, disappeared into a hole in the flesh and ended at the bone, while another bit of wire came out and went back over the ear.' The precise technical description of this horrifying dream is particularly gruesome, like the extreme vividness of *Metamorphosis* in which the suffering and death of a commercial traveller, changed over-night into a sort of beetle or louse, but doomed to keep his human consciousness, are described with a cool clarity that makes this one of the most bloodcurdling stories in all literature. Here the 'law' assails its unsuspecting victim in a particularly cruel way, but perhaps this is only to unmask the family (which represents the world of the heartless panthers) as the real enemy. Another diary entry suggests that this too is connected with a whole complex of Kafka's experiences: in it he notes how, in the bosom of his family, he had to put up with the critical remarks of an uncle apropos of some lines he had written (he obviously gives them much too much importance): 'I went on sitting there, bending over my now useless page, but all the same I had been driven out of the company at one blow, my uncle's criticism reverberated in me with almost real significance and even within the warmth of the family I got a glimpse of the cold space of our world, which I would have to warm with a fire I had still to find.' In the *Meditations* this 'fire' is viewed with an incomparable wisdom which again reminds one of all Stifter's disciplined restraint: 'Art flies round the truth but with the definite intention of not getting burned in it. Its talent is for finding a place in the dark void where the beam of the light can be powerfully intercepted, although it was not recognisable beforehand.'

The reflections from the eternal light which art seeks, fall on life as fragments of an unknown whole. If one tries to reconnoitre the writer's position from his notes and sketches, it is almost understandable that most, and the most important, of his works remained fragments. But in this case fragmentariness means something different from merely not being finished. It is hardly a question of finding out how this or that story Kafka began would have gone on. In the ordinary sense, of course, they did not go on but were lost in the darkness of their immense environment, but their meaning immediately goes on in another story which begins to shape itself until it too breaks off somewhere. The subject of the stories—the solitary man's struggle to understand the law and the way he is broken by its immeasurable power—goes on all the time. Perhaps it is most shatteringly presented in the oppressive story *In the Penal Colony*, where the opposition between grace and law, which does not often shine through so clearly in Kafka, is captured in a mysterious, hovering intermediate state.

16

BASIC PRINCIPLES OF A NEW THEORY
OF MUSICAL AESTHETICS

THERE is very little point in thinking about musical aesthetics
and trying to construct a new system if the term is taken to
mean merely 'the doctrine of what is beautiful in music'. We
do not have to accept this limitation of the term 'aesthetic' and
burden ourselves from the very beginning with the task of
making problematical value-judgments. The Greek dictionary
tells us that αἴδνησις means 'sensation, sensual perception,
observing, recognising, understanding'. It is in this sense that
aesthetics are of interest, because it is important to recast our
sensual perceptions of modern music in the form of intellectual
perceptions and to raise observation to the level of recognition
and understanding. In fact, viewed from the outside, the problem of modern music is one of recognition and understanding,
because its inner, technical problem is one of form. For in the
aesthetic sense, form is a pre-requisite of recognition; formless
content is inconceivable and consequently also unrecognisable.
So if new music strikes us as obscure, the reason is, obviously,
that we do not understand its forms. The whole point and content of musical aesthetics, is learning to understand these forms.

But it is more important to establish something else first:
how far theoretical research in general is capable of throwing
light on musical problems. First of all one needs to be convinced
that all man's intellectual activities are homogeneous and speak
with one voice. I do not mean that they are, as it were, parallel
and comparable in tendency. It would not be enough merely
to assume, as Oswald Spengler does, that they are all mutually

dependent, in the sense that each form of expression is sympto-matic of the others. It can, of course, be said that Beethoven's music and Kant's philosophy are symbols of each other, be-cause both correspond to a certain intellectual attitude. But such parallels are not enough to prove the justification of using thought-processes as norms against which to measure artistic processes any more than the idea that music is the expression of a consciousness existing outside it and determined by its material. This idea, which is older and more widespread, has led to the 'content-and-expression' aesthetics which satisfy the listener by giving him credible associations as he listens to the work—whether they are utterly naïve, concrete and descrip-tive, as in a piece imitating a sleigh-ride, or a little more sublime, as in a symphonic composition where the great feelings con-jured up can be identified by reference to the programme sup-plied with it. Due to these 'expressive aesthetics', the average listener's ability to experience is totally unused to acting without such crutches; and the public's rejection of modern music largely stems from the fact that this primitive association-mechanism is not applicable to it, while the other organs of comprehension have atrophied.

What I mean by the homogeneity of man's intellectual ac-tivities is not merely the fact that they are related symbolically or in expression; I mean that their inmost essence is analogous, that they are more or less identical. It is indeed feasible to *think* about music, according to this theory, because music itself is a form of thinking, so that the analytical thought-process with which we examine musical things is completely identical with the intuitive thought-process which leads to the production of a musical work; and indeed the distinction between the 'analy-tical' and 'intuitive' thought-processes only represents a real difference in so far as a piece of music must exist before it can be thought about. The word 'intuitive' is in no way meant to

130

suggest that the musical creative process is a matter of the piece miraculously springing fully-fledged out of its creator's head. I call it 'intuitive' to express the fact that the means of the musical creative process cannot be grasped directly in conceptual terms; that is they are not basically accessible to the means of verbal language. It is in this sense that I hope the apparently contradictory term 'intuitive thought-process' will be permitted and understood. But despite the distinction, the thought-process with which we grasp and understand a musical event must be identical with the thought-process itself; only the medium is different—one takes place in verbal language, the other in sound-language. Let me express this even more concretely (and one must make oneself as clear as possible so as to avoid still more confusion). Suppose, in analysing a certain piece, for example the following passage:

I say: 'Here there is a modulation from C major to A flat minor achieved by interpreting the tonic triad of C major as the dominant triad of F minor, without actually introducing the F minor chord; it is merely felt to anticipate the A flat in the dominant seventh on C; the (omitted) F minor triad is followed by its sub-mediant—D flat major—whose third is flattened, whereupon the D flat minor triad this produces is interpreted as the sub-dominant of A flat minor, whose tonic follows in its first inversion and is firmly established by means of a cadence.' At first sight I have produced a rather complicated thought-process about a little passage that might occur anywhere in Schubert and sounds very simple. If I say that this thought-

131

process is identical with the one carried out by the composer when he created this passage, I do not mean that he sat down and said to himself: 'Now I shall take a C major triad and interpret it . . .' etc., but that he thought directly in triads, dominant sevenths and so on—those were his medium of thought, just as ours, for the moment, is the terms with which we are trying to paraphrase these musical means. But his thought-process, entirely enclosed within the medium of musical means that exist only for themselves, *must* be identical with our thought-process, entirely confined to the linguistic medium, for the simple reason that we cannot read anything technical into the musical process or deduce anything from it apart from what is actually in it. The fact that the musical means are locked in their sphere and cannot be reached by verbal language, the awed amazement that even such a bold and intensive concept as 'triad' cannot produce a single real one, while the composer, apparently thoughtless and often notoriously tongue-tied, can toss off not only triads, but much more complicated structures—all this obscures the fact that the processes which result in a piece of music are thought-processes too, but in a system of elements that verbal language can only grasp *via* terms and concepts, *via* the names (triad, tonic, etc.) that we give these elements—names which are by no means the elements themselves. A parallel from the sphere of verbal language will make this even clearer. However astute my thinking, it cannot tell me what this or that word is in English. And yet when I hear even very poorly-endowed Englishmen talking English fluently, I cannot doubt that exactly the same thought-processes underlie their apparently instinctive use of English as underlie any other language, and that I can reproduce them *via* a translation. Of course it is not the same thing when I translate a sentence from English into German, for the actual words are obviously entirely different, but something about the two versions is more than alike—

132

it is the same—and that is the thought, which must be identical; otherwise mine would be a bad translation, because I would have read into the original something that was not there.

Recognising that music too is a thought-process is also a guarantee of its autonomy. This is particularly important with regard to the main concern of these thoughts about musical aesthetics. I have shown elsewhere that by sticking to *espressivo*, modern music (with which we are specially concerned) was forced to transform the sound-language, the actual material. So we must first try to explain and justify this change: later we shall be able to see what kind of a state the new sound-language, as such, is in. So long as we fail to recognise the musical process as a thought-process carried out in a self-contained medium exclusive to music, it is bound to remain tied to other kinds of values outside itself. It then appears to be an expression of historical, psychological or other factors and is unrecognisable as a musical process. As a result it remains impossible to explain the transformation of music, for it is obviously dictated by arbitrary influences of a heterogeneous kind and without any inner logic. This line of reasoning leads to the ideas that an age full of discord uses more dissonances in its music, a serene, peace-loving man writes more 'harmonious' music, and so on and so forth. Even if few people would admit to holding this vulgar view of musical aesthetics, secretly it is much deeper rooted than might be thought, and this sometimes emerges involuntarily. From this point it is only a step to the idea that one could make the age seem more harmonious by writing more tonal music, and that if only discontented types could be restrained from composing, the annoying and confusing transformation of the sound-language could be stopped. First, then, we must make it plain that music is autonomous with regard to other fields; only then can we grasp the importance of the changes taking place in the musical sphere itself.

But, on the other hand, we must also find a standpoint from which we can judge musical value as such, independent of its expression in one sound-language or another, in this style or that style. Of course our ultimate aim is to explain and legitimise modern music, but if we confined ourselves to it alone, the result would be a very partisan apology which would prove nothing apart from its immediate thesis. So far all theories of musical aesthetics have tended to be apologies, intellectual systems designed to defend a certain musical style. One could, of course, set up an aesthetic theory in defence of modern music too, as has already been done on occasion. But any apology that goes no further than its immediate subject has the disadvantage of not applying outside that field; in another field it can justifiably be disputed—in short it is only valid on the basis of assumptions which are exactly those it is setting out to prove and defend. To express something really valid one must look for assumptions of a more general kind than the one which the thought-structure is built to protect. In other words, we need to sketch out an aesthetic theory which, in its turn, is autonomous with regard to the historical facts of particular sound-language areas, particular styles. It must be so framed that these fields—the field of Gregorian chant, or of church styles, of major-minor tonality or atonality—figure in it as special cases within a general theory.

On this point there is a distinction between aesthetics and 'practical theory'. The aesthetic theory we are now steering towards is the result of analysing and interpreting the thought-scheme common to all the individual cases of musical thought-processes—it is a presentation of this thought-scheme, originally only musical, in the medium of verbal language. It claims validity for all the different ways of putting the musical thought-process into practice. Practical theory, on the other hand, is a synthetic, systematic presentation of the musical thought-processes which together constitute a certain style, a concrete sound-language area. But the important thing about it is that what the 'theory' puts forward as the rule to be learned is not the result of a norm existing outside and before music; it simply observes the existing practice in a certain style and recommends it for imitation. In other words: it is not that a theory of tonal harmony was written first, that it demonstrated all the definitions and rules of tonal music in an abstract way, and that composers then began to work according to these rules. Quite the reverse: tonal compositions were written for a long time and various experiments were made before observation and comparison of these works gradually revealed a series of characteristics which appeared regularly and could finally be listed as rules. From this point it was possible to pass these rules on in teaching, and demand that they must be followed if the result was to be real tonal music. For the rules contained the conditions that had to be fulfilled in order that the definition of tonality could be applied to the created work. Above all, in the age of the theory of evolution and belief in personal progress, the natural urge to declare creation definitive and binding hardened into the idea that tonal music was the highest fulfilment of all musical possibilities, and that everything before had merely been leading up to it, so that 'theory' ceased to be a practical method for creating certain musical structures on certain assumptions and became a sort of fetish, a code of laws laid down for all time by nature. In particular, the overtone-theory made it possible to show a link between harmonic doctrine and science, and a musical text-book could begin by showing the relationships between vibration-figures before passing on to real musical considerations. Consequently the 'theory' of tonality seemed more or less impossible to dethrone in the eyes of an age brought up to feel awe for science. Even as radical a thinker as Schoenberg did not always succeed in throwing off the scientific spectre, and he thought he should relate even his most independent ideas to the overtone-theory, which, though undoubtedly correct scientifically, is largely irrelevant to music.

To return to the parallel with verbal language, a musical 'theory' is comparable with a language grammar which is based on observations of the living language, but presents these observations in a form and synthetic pattern that enables the pupil to use them as a method for producing new structures in the language. This is not likely to make anyone believe that the language was actually invented by the author and must never be altered, enlarged or changed in any particular. What I am aiming at is a study of music comparable with a philology that indicates the basic elements of language—as it were, what is necessary if a form of expression is to be called language at all —regardless of all the individual presentations of the general language-element in the individual cases of individual languages.

Obviously then, we cannot work synthetically, like 'theory'. Nor can we, as at first sight seems the obvious course, start from the atom which is clearly the common basis of all music, the single note. However much we turn and twist it, it cannot tell us how music emerges from a multiplication of itself. We shall only come up against the famous overtones (analytically this time, instead of synthetically) and they will either lead us to the absolute sovereignty of major-minor tonality, which cannot answer our purpose of finding a theory that also covers other types of sound-language, or show that the overtones cannot constitute major-minor tonality or any other musical system. If, then, we cannot work outwards synthetically from the atom we shall have to start analytically from some kind of *totality*.

It is only recently that the entity idea has begun to play a crucial role in music. In his most interesting book *Individualpsychologie im Musikunterricht und in der Musikerziehung* (Leipzig,

136

1931) the Viennese music-teacher Leonhard Deutsch makes much play with the entity-concept which in general he derives from orientation towards certain purposes, in the usage of individual psychology, instead of inquiring into the causes, which would have to be done analytically. Another function of the entity-concept emerges from *Grundlagen einer autonomen Musikästhetik* by the Swiss composer and theorist Ernst Georg Wolff (Strasburg, 1934) which directly inspired this essay. The entity from which Wolff starts is the interval. He, too, observes that musical circumstances cannot be developed from the single note, and he sees the original cell of the musical process as the two-note tension of the interval with its tendency to change into another tension-relationship when a third note enters. Wolff worked out the concept of autonomy in musical aesthetics particularly clearly. But the functions of the entity-concept that are fundamental to our enquiry may be found in Christian von Ehrenfels' article 'Uber Gestaltqualitäten' in the *Vierteljahrschrift für wissenschaftliche Philosophie*, 1890 (14th yr., no III). This is an examination from a psychological standpoint of the conditions under which, and the way in which, we are able to perceive apparently complex and highly organised phenomena, such as melodies, etc., as wholes.

I have become convinced that the entity-concept could be fruitfully applied to the sphere of music, but I think that so far, attempts have not got to the heart of the matter because they have not got beyond entities of a formal or peripheral kind. Here the terminology needs elucidation. I call my method— using an entity as the starting point for analysis—analytical because it should show that the parts (which one proceeds to study after studying the whole) are a function of the whole which exists *a priori*, and not that the whole is the sum of the parts. Any approach based on this last attitude ought rightly to be called synthetic. Now, in a sense, even the old harmony-doctrine was based on entities such as the key-concept which it saw represented in the scale. But not only is the scale presented as something composite, built up out of intervals—neither the scale nor the key is a true, final entity in the sense in which we must use this term. If we want to study the entity really consistently we must first look at music itself—in other words, at what is stored in the works and what reaches the ear when they are performed. This is obviously the essence, the living flesh of music; all other ideas are derivative, partial, judgments from particular points of view, the results of particular attitudes. To go no further, we can easily see that neither the key nor the scale, this chord nor that chord, this or that principle of construction and order, are basic; all these are elements to which many musical phenomena can be reduced if one accepts certain assumptions. When I hear the funeral march from the *Eroica* I can explain all the musical events in it in terms of elements belonging to the C minor concept. I can even show that the key of C minor is grasped as an entity by the listener, even if he has no idea of its theoretical character, for it is one of the conditions necessary for the piece to be experienced as a unified whole. But this is nevertheless a formal, secondary type of entity, for it never emerges as such; it must be deduced from the work by applying certain points of view. What is the entity that would satisfy our needs? As I have already indicated it is the 'musical thought', and I will now go into this in more detail.

The term 'musical idea' is much used by Schoenberg and his pupils, and this inspired me to go more deeply into the concept and use a precise definition to draw conclusions which do not stand out clearly from more approximate, comparative formulae. First we must make one thing absolutely clear: we are dealing with the *musical* thought, that is, a thought that belongs exclusively to the sphere of music and can only be expressed with musical means, which is identical with its realisation in musical material and cannot be separated from it; it cannot be encountered, described, defined or even named in verbal language. It is necessary to get this quite clear because experience teaches that the average person, under the influence of expressive aesthetics, has only to hear the words 'musical thought' to imagine that this is a metaphor, that music expresses a thought, or rather a feeling, that exists outside itself. By 'musical thought' I mean something that is contained entirely in the musical medium and that we can only perceive through that medium, without the intervention of extra-musical considerations or translation into another medium. The 'musical thought' is to the verbal thought (which is by definition a thought in *terms*) —as the original of immediacy is to its concrete definitions in the logical sphere; it completes its realisation in the pre-logical sphere just as that of verbal thought does in the logical sphere, which is why the parallel with verbal language can throw so much light on the process.

It may perhaps appear that 'musical thought' is just another way of saying 'musical theme'; but in fact the idea of the 'musical thought' is much broader and less narrowly concrete than the idea of the theme, by which is usually meant a musical pattern exposed to certain technical processes of composition. The thought is a wider category whose bearing we can perhaps best explain by another parallel with verbal language. Just as we recognise a thought in verbal language by the fact that it represents the main content of a sentence, so we recognise the musical thought by the 'wholeness' of the musical sentence it forms. This is open to the objection that it makes our decisions dependent on very subjective factors. For there is no one right answer to the question of where a musical sentence begins or ends, or what it looks like; the logic which governs the expression of a thought in verbal language does not function in music with even approximate precision. There can be no doubt that the sentence: 'The elephant has a trunk' is not complete without the word 'trunk', but in music one is often faced with insoluble questions. However, these are not disposed of or even made easier to solve by speaking of the theme, the period or the like, instead of the thought; they are only transferred to the purely technical sphere. How one can grasp one musical thought or another in its concrete form is less important here than the knowledge that it really represents the entity which no form or commentary can give music or deduce from it; it is, rather, the inmost essence of music itself. There cannot be any doubt that it is the totality of the thought that we grasp in listening, not the sum of a number of individual notes, nor the concrete presentation of a key-consciousness, nor the absence of it. Admittedly, all these things go to make up the thought and are consequently demonstrable, just as the sentence about the elephant may be viewed as the sum of its letters, as the relationship of vowels and consonants, a logical construction or a grammatical phenomenon, because all these things are in it. But the entity we perceive first in both cases is undoubtedly the thought. Without getting involved in endless casuistry it may be said that the 'musical thought' is what conditions and fills a musical *Gestalt*. The musical *Gestalt* is the way the thought manifests itself in musical material, but I want to avoid the word 'form' because I need to use it later for another concept. However, we must beware of seeing anything dualistic in this pair of terms, thought-Gestalt, as though the thought were something existing in itself and being expressed, symbolised or copied in the musical Gestalt. The thought is identical with its Gestalt, each can replace the other, and we have only introduced the idea of the Gestalt to define that of the thought, not to provide an opposite to it.

Purely genetically, the 'musical thought' is subordinate to an entity of a more general kind that I should like to call the 'idea'. It can be more or less identified with the total conception of the work, which contains factors relating to both form and content. Since creative impulses of all kinds find expression in this, it is the only one of the entities we shall consider which also has a certain extra-musical content. The idea is, so to speak, the top layer of the creative process, the one nearest to extra-musical matter, from which it receives impulses of the most varied kinds, according to its arrangement; it then passes these on, in a completely transmuted, assimilated form, to the musical interior. It is for the psychology of the creative process to investigate this layer. Julius Bahles is the man who recognised it as such and isolated it from both general psychology and musical aesthetics; he has thrown much light on these questions in several smaller studies and a longer work, *Der Musikalische Schaffensprozess* (Leipzig, 1936). The general creative intentions are contained in the idea-layer; they are always accompanied by musical conceptions whose indeterminacy and generality distinguish them from thoughts. The idea, then, is an entity of a higher order, but it is not a suitable point from which to start our examination because it is general, and also because it does not reach the listener directly, as he listens, but can only be recognised by synthetically grasping the thoughts in which it is expressed. For the time being, let us stick to the thought and its Gestalt.

When we consider the medium in which the Gestalt appears, the material out of which it is made, we must always bear in mind that we are starting from a *tabula rasa* and know nothing of keys, scales, keynotes, consonances, dissonances, chords, or anything of the sort. We are more or less in the position of a dumb man who first has certain general ideas and then concrete thoughts he wants to communicate, but still only knows that there is some kind of acoustic equipment at his disposal. The acoustic equipment at the disposal of the thinker of musical thoughts is the continuum of notes which we hear when a motor runs or a siren wails—a limited chain with an infinity of links. If the thought is to become Gestalt in this medium, it must become a language—in our case, a sound-language. Note that an insoluble unity is emerging before our eyes: it is the thought's inherent need to present itself which creates the language—it would not exist without thoughts. On the other hand without language the thought is not only incommunicable, but in the strictly literal sense, unthinkable. For us the most important factor in considering sound-language is the realisation that it is not an unequivocal system existing in its own right, rooted in the acoustic equipment and explicable in terms of its natural character, but an organ and at the same time the first creation of the free, sovereign thought. According to this view the elements that constitute a tone-language are still not elements with a special constructive power of their own. We are still nowhere near key-notes, scales and other principles of construction; no arrangements of this kind are assumed beforehand, only the thought now looking for the way to its most complete realisation and creating the necessary organs out of the sound-equipment available. What constitutes tone-language, in our sense, is rather a general but characteristic structure conferred on the raw material by the thought. If we consider some of the thoughts characteristic of the thinking of classical music, for example (the main theme of the *Eroica*, the finale of Mozart's symphony in G minor, etc.), it is clear that one of the essential melodic elements is the tonal triad. It is also clear that a thought of this kind will give the raw material quite a different structure from that given by such thoughts as appear in, say, Schoenberg's piano pieces. Partly because the artists of any one age, any one cultural and geographical community, tend to have thoughts of a similar kind, and partly because one specially strong mind will give a lead to the thinking of many others, one particular tone-language will become valid for considerable periods and areas. It is not the other way round—that composers use it because it is valid for some unknown reason (perhaps because it is taught in the academies). The thought is always sovereign, and the new thought creates a new language for itself.

The thing I am calling the tone-language is not the same as style; the style embraces far less, for various styles are accommodated within the range of validity of one tone-language. The tone-language of major-minor tonality, for example, a living language from about 1600 to the present day, comprises many very different styles, as we all know. Hence one should not speak of an atonal style, but an atonal language, within which various styles are perfectly possible, and indeed already observable up to a certain point.

In creating the tone-language the thought has given the raw material a certain structure; now it has to use these structural elements so as to develop its Gestalt further. To give the Gestalt solidity the first thing necessary is articulation, an alternation of elements—a disjunctive, 'de-composing' function. To take up the parallel with verbal language again, we have now reached the point where the oppositions between consonants and vowels, the differences between gutturals, labials and nasals emerge, where syllables can be given different values by different accentuation, where thesis and antithesis take on a meaning, and so on. I will group all these functions together under the name of 'articulation'. In the sphere of tone-language the elements that fulfil these functions are of a very related kind: first there are the processes of tension and release, realised in the difference of character between dissonance and consonance—dissonance representing the higher degree of tension and consonance the lower degree, so that there is a power-incline between the two. The differences in tension lead to an articulation according to accent and emphasis; the alternation of thesis and arsis creates the infinite variety of rhythms which all have an articulating, cutting-up character, until the phrase (the musical sentence) emerges from the interaction of this highly subtle system of weight-distributions on the most various bases.

Again I must emphasise that according to this view the difference between consonance and dissonance, for example, is not something existing in nature but a creation of thought, which uses a possibility in natural material to create its Gestalt. This is of vital importance, because it purges the dissonance of its magical character as an inviolable physical discovery. Obviously the type and character of the thought are responsible for the appearance of the dissonance- and consonance-concepts it fashions according to its needs. This also explains, very satisfactorily, why in musical history the concepts of consonance and dissonance have meant very different things at different times—a fact impossible to square with the part-of-nature theory. As the sovereignty of the thought has not hitherto been recognised, the last definition of it has always been extolled as a fact of nature, so as to stifle any new form at birth. That the ears accommodate themselves to each new treatment of the musical elements is obvious, according to our argument, for 'it is the mind which builds itself a body'.

The alternating sequence of articulating elements, mainly individualising the thought, defining its limits, giving it a memorable contour and characteristic shape, produce an opposite force which is not so essential to the individual thought's Gestalt as its clear, plastic articulation, but which is almost always created along with the articulation. I shall call these elements relating-forces; unlike the articulating ones, they are constructive, conjunctive—they collect things together. Their most primitive form is repetition, which even occurs, at its lowest level, when articulating elements merely alternate, so that, for example, an unstressed element has to recur after a

144

stressed one. Higher elements of this kind are connections—partial correspondences between elements that, as wholes, are differentiated from each other: repetition again, therefore, but only with regard to some, not all, aspects of the element. Variations—keeping certain factors and changing others (especially inversion)—keeping the intervals and changing, i.e. reversing, the sequence, retrograde and inverted forms, imitation, repetition at the same or a different pitch while simultaneously continuing the first entry of the element imitated—augmentation and diminution—keeping the Gestalt while proportionately altering the rhythmic structure, and so on. All these things are known by the collective term of motivic relationships (connections); their meaning and consequence is to produce coherence among the individual Gestalts created by articulation.

Incidentally, Schoenberg has often—most recently in the article 'Problems of Harmony' in *Modern Music* (New York, May 1934)—made similar references to articulating and combining elements in music. However, my theory goes further than Schoenberg's. He sees tonality as a medium specially privileged and adapted to guarantee the fulfilment of these functions. According to my argument, tonality is something that only emerges, with a certain quality of musical thought, from the thoughts' complete transformation of the raw material at the level of articulation and relation, whereupon it can be deduced from the finished pattern. With other types of thoughts and, consequently, articulation and relation working in different ways, it does not emerge at all, but its absence, as such, is by no means a defect. It will be seen that the relating aspects are not so indispensable when the thought is becoming Gestalt as those of articulation, for there are many, many musical formations in which several, or often nearly all, of these relationships are missing; but we cannot conceive of any kind of music which could do without the articulating component parts. It will also be seen that the relating forces are no longer so directly, as it were vitally, linked with the musical raw material; they are no longer simply necessary structure and the very first elementary possibility of shaping the material; they already represent a higher intellectual shaping, modelling, defining. The power of thought which first made the raw material into an articulated tone-language, now provides its Gestalt with the more refined organs of connection, relationship.

It is these, above all, that enable the thought to grow into 'form'. All the elements grouped within the concept of relation make it possible to link several thoughts, which is necessary to create form in the true sense. The possibility of linking them rests on the extent to which certain elements can be related to each other, on the possibility of recognising the element of one thought in the element of another. In its turn this possibility exists when something of the first element recurs in the second one, whether it is repeated literally or varied in a freer or less free way. Of course the individual thought has its form, but I have been calling it its Gestalt, so as to keep 'form' for the coherent structure.

This is where the music's relationship to its period comes into play. Schoenberg's dictum 'Thought has no period' was meant in quite another sense, but we could apply it to our own uses (the fact that it fits here, too, might be said to prove its truth and language's power of going on being right even when one twists its words). Of course the thought in its musical Gestalt has a very real duration—and with a thought such as the adagio, a long duration, at that—but in the higher sense it is a unit, a musical atom, an entity which is not made up of single elements, but has created elements out of its quality of totality. So in a way the single thought does not take up any musical time; one has only counted 'one', however many bars or seconds of real time have passed. We only count 'two', and time only begins to pass, when the new thought arrives. But here the form, which consists of the linking of several thoughts, begins to grow. At the same time, form is also an entity-concept, which can be seen from the psychology of creation. It is hardly possible that musical form is the result of a composer's having a thought, writing it down, and then wondering whether he can combine it with other thoughts, and with how many, so as to make a larger form. But we have already seen how form already exists as an entity above that of the thought—as the 'idea', which determines the creative process, in a general, outline way, even before the thought. So we have come round full circle, in that the thought, in its completest musical incarnation, the form, returns to the idea and so to the threshold of the extra-musical, human world, on which it has an effect in its way, when music is heard, accepted and understood by people.

The value of this whole approach (which I have only outlined here) is that it makes it possible to describe and classify all the phenomena that constitute a work and are perceptible in it, without claiming or introducing any one constructive scheme, such as modality, major-minor tonality or atonality, without its being necessary to accept any one of these. The suspicion which is dawning on the contemporary musician more and more in his practical music-making and of which there are even traces in recent theoretical writings—the suspicion that music does not begin with the scale but ends with it—proves to be completely correct. We have never come up against scales, never missed their absence and never found it necessary to introduce them. Music is not based on scales, which are created by particular tone-languages or tonalities; it is the thought that creates the tone-language from which you can derive a scale if you want one. This may be done if one wants to write a practical 'theory', a grammar of the tone-language, a collection of instructions on how to use its vocabulary—but it is very questionable whether even that is as essential as has always been thought.

We have done what we set out to do—constructed a musical theory not dependent on the data of particular tone-languages and embracing all concrete phenomena. As required, the separate tone-languages appear as individual cases within a generally valid thought-process which, by association with the thought-system that covers all possible verbal languages, might be christened 'musical logic'. This, but only this, can be called 'musical logic': the elementary categories of a purely formal kind which we have spoken of and which the free, sovereign thought fills with a limitless variety of life. This 'musical logic' is the incarnation of the pre-logical state of thought, carried out through general logic. The term 'musical logic' has hitherto been misused by pedants to mean the ordinary general logic which governs every system of rules, including that of a particular one such as classical harmony, in their attempts to prove the inviolability of the system they have at heart. So perhaps it is better not to use the term for the time being. It is enough if we call ours a system of musical aesthetics because we have seen that the categories it demands are necessary for an acoustical process to be recognised as a musical one. This system is shown in diagram form opposite.

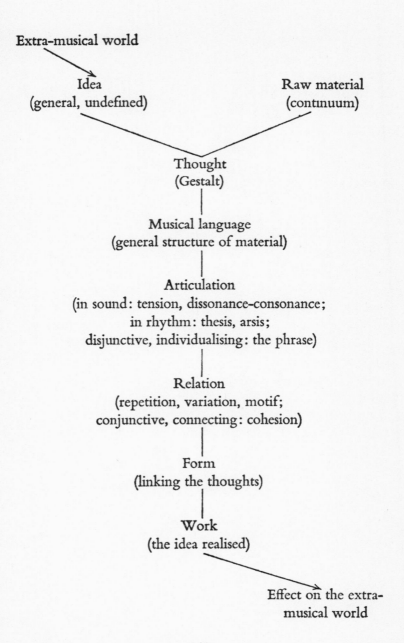

Extra-musical world

Idea
(general, undefined)

Raw material
(continuum)

Thought
(Gestalt)

Musical language
(general structure of material)

Articulation
(in sound: tension, dissonance-consonance;
in rhythm: thesis, arsis;
disjunctive, individualising: the phrase)

Relation
(repetition, variation, motif;
conjunctive, connecting: cohesion)

Form
(linking the thoughts)

Work
(the idea realised)

Effect on the extra-
musical world

17

MUSIC FOR ETERNITY

ONE of the entertainments with which the coming World Exhibition at New York has already tried to attract the attention due to it, is the burying of a large torpedo-like tube deep in the earth. This tube weighs eight hundred pounds and contains samples of contemporary civilisation designed to give an amazed posterity, five thousand years hence, evidence of what we considered worth preserving for it. Scientists have taken pains to ensure that the tube is proof against every possible catastrophe that may occur in the intervening period. So far nothing has been said as to how information about the existence and site of this tube will be kept alive for five thousand years, but some trouble must surely be taken over this if one is pessimistic enough—as the originators of the idea seem to be—to admit the possibility that after five thousand years nothing will be left of our civilisation but what is contained in this tube.

I have not got a precise list of the treasures to be buried, but reports reassure us that such important objects as poker-dice will not be forgotten. Naturally music forms only a very small part of the eight hundred pounds of culture. It is represented by the following articles: a miniature score of Sibelius' *Finlandia*, Sousa's march *The Stars and Stripes for Ever*, and a work entitled *Flat Foot Floozie* by three composers, Bud Green, Slim Gaillard and Sam Stewart. In addition there are photographs—of Toscanini on the conductor's rostrum, a string quartet playing, couples dancing in a club and a few other illustrations of our musical culture.

What the good finders of these objects will make of them it is impossible to conjecture. When you consider what difficulties we have in deciphering a musical manuscript no more than a thousand years old, although we have much more source material to refer to than one ceremonially preserved tube, there seems little hope that Sousa's masterpiece will be successfully resurrected after five thousand years. But even if wonderful archaeological expertise should succeed in interpreting the music correctly, despite the lack of all other sources, and even if these people of the distant future should in some inconceivable way be able to assess the value of this carefully preserved music with complete accuracy, the destruction of all other music would almost be less regrettable for its own sake than because posterity could only get even an approximate picture of present-day civilisation with the aid of what is *not* in the tube.

Finlandia is a completely conventional work by the Finnish composer who has, for some reason hard to understand, won great popularity with the Anglo-Saxon peoples. The Sousa piece is a patriotic march for the use of American military bands. What *Flat Foot Floozie* is, is probably known only to the patrons of the club whose photograph will survive along with it. But they too will have forgotten it by next year, and it seems reasonable to doubt whether the Americans of 6939 will be very curious about it.

Our only hope of saving our reputation is that posterity will not be able to read the music. Perhaps they will take Toscanini for a kind of wizard waving a magic wand, and develop a theory that the photograph of the string quartet represents Messrs Sousa, Green, Gaillard and Stewart engaged in some prehistoric sawing activity.

How lucky that the Greeks never hit on the idea of burying a tube! We can think the very best of them. When one thinks of the cultural mish-mash in New York, one almost feels that the barbarians who set fire to the library of Alexandria did more to preserve classical culture than the manager of the Olympic Games would have done had he buried a little fire-proof, earthquake-proof, poison-proof box containing all the pop songs of Alcibiades' day.

18

THE IVORY TOWER

IT is a matter of general agreement that professional musicians who cultivate so-called serious music are high-brow and long-haired individuals, and this is being held against them. The reason usually brought forward in support of such criticism is that the music written and performed by those individuals cannot be enjoyed by the common man because of its complexity and lack of emotional appeal. There may be something to that, but I seem to have observed that still more irritating than the music itself is the way in which those musicians are wont to talk about their trade. The average music lover, if he has the desire to become vocal about his experience, is inclined to describe in the first place the feelings which he thought were aroused by the music, and in doing so he uses comparisons, images and metaphors, substituting for the true cause of his emotional reaction, namely the music he had just heard, such objects and concepts of the world of reality, as in his opinion are liable to create similar emotional reactions. As a rule, he does not know that he is speaking in metaphors, since the musical substance itself appears to him so elusive that he comes to think that those objects and concepts of the outside world are actually in the music, transformed into sound by some miraculous process. In most cases the layman will not even have the impression that the musical substance is elusive, he will simply not notice that it exists at all. If he thinks that the mood which seems to emanate from a piece of music is similar to that in which he might find himself in a moon-lit night, he will briefly assume that the composer had been in exactly that mood while writing the music, that he was more or less consciously intent upon communicating that mood, and that the mood of the composer was caused by moonlight shining upon him at the time of the creative process.

Put in such terms, the interpretation by which the average listener may try to explain his experience sounds fairly silly, and it is so easy to ridicule it, that something should be said in its defense. The main justification for this state of mind is its obvious sincerity. It is quite certain that in most cases our music lover does not make up his associations, he really experiences them, so that we will have to admit that some inherent reason for those associations must obtain. Incredible amounts of ink have been spilled throughout the centuries with the aim of elucidating the relationships of music to the outside and inside world. Aesthetics and psychology have been delving into the mysteries of that problem, and each period in the history of the human mind has presented solutions of them, according to the angle from which the various thinkers looked upon the nature of that mind. Without going into the details of those highly controversial theories, it may be safe to state that music, like anything else in our surroundings, be it made by man or by nature, has certain features that are identifiable with expressive qualities. Without paying much attention to it, we are constantly making such identifications. We are wont to call a certain mountain threatening, because of its shape and outline, although we would be at a loss to explain what it threatens; some other landscape appears serene and smiling, although it really does not smile, and we are not thinking perhaps that people living in that landscape are necessarily serene and smiling, for we know that murder and arson may be committed in any kind of surroundings. We are, of course, in the habit of interpreting physiognomic features of people we see as expressive of their character and moods, and students of graphology will tell you that any trait of a person's handwriting has expressive significance, independent from the intentions of the writer. The essential point in all these cases is that we are making those associative identifications basically by intuition. Our faculty of making them may become more extensive and surer of the results through practice and experience, but it seems to exist in every human being from the outset. Of course, there is no reason to believe that musical phenomena ought to be excluded from that kind of expressive interpretation, and probably most musicians will be ready to grant you that.

However, the true musician will not stop there, and the more initiated he is by talent and training, the less deserving of interest this complex of expressive associations will appear to him. Where the average listener is pleased by the music's reminding him of a moon-lit night on the seashore, the musician will express his delight at the delicacy of the harmonic process, the smoothness of modulation, the subtlety of the melodic curve and such like details. When the layman is satisfied with the general excitement prevailing in a piece of music that purports to describe a battle, the musician will appraise the ingenuity of rhythmic combinations, the distribution of metric stresses, the climax plan and other seemingly technical affairs. If such a divergence of attention seems irksome enough to the layman, it becomes particularly annoying in those numerous cases in which the music did not appeal to the common man at all, because his habitual associative mechanism was not set in motion by it, whereas the musician is still raving about structure and texture, phrase construction and counterpoint, thematic development and similar accomplishments. It is here that angry voices can be heard to the effect that musicians who indulge in that sort of talk are preventing the true nature of music, because they approach it intellectually instead of relying upon their intuition and sentiments.

Now in the first place it seems rather strange that anybody should be blamed for using his brains on no matter what subject, since man so far has set a certain pride in his having brains. Secondly, musicians exposed to that sort of criticism are frequently somewhat puzzled as to what it really means, for to them their own attitude toward music appears so natural and spontaneous that they feel that if there is anything objectionably intellectual in this whole matter, it is rather the other approach, the so-called intuitive and emotional. They feel that in talking about music in musical terms they have the most desirable clear-cut and immediate contact with the object itself, whereas the introduction of moonlight and other extraneous subject matter looks very much like an intellectual detour. No matter what the undeniable relationship of those extraneous concepts with music may be, they are brought into the discussion from the outside and will remain there forever, affording but little intelligence on the musical process itself, in which the musician is so passionately interested.

As I mentioned in the beginning, musicians who entertain this attitude are frequently called long-haired, especially by people who have trouble in pronouncing the work 'intellectual', which in itself is a part of the high-brow vocabulary. The fact, however, is that especially those musicians who are wont to talk about music in musical terms, have adopted a long time ago the usual civilian haircut, and if you ever see a musician with that curly mane so familiar from 19th century portraits of virtuosos, you may be sure that he will be much more inclined toward the moonlight attitude than those of his colleagues who visit barbershops regularly.

Anyhow, the abode of the long-haired intellectuals is known among their opponents as the Ivory Tower. I am quite sure that nobody so far has seen a tower made of ivory, but the general impression evoked by this metaphorical term is that of a possibly attractive, but at any rate very expensive edifice, considering the proverbial scarcity of the material. Another factor that may, too, come under consideration in using this image is the brittleness of ivory, so that a tower constructed from such matter would be a rather delicate object and therefore likely to be built in remote spots, safe from the hazards of heavy traffic. These are indeed the elements underlying the now common use of the metaphor: the artist who is blamed for his egotistic, esoteric brooding is also suspected of what has become known as escapism. His interests are characterised as luxury—that is what the ivory obviously stands for—and he is supposed to be so infatuated with his love for intellectual luxury that he despises the coarse reality of life as it goes on in the market place and prefers to erect his precious but fragile abode in the safety of solitude.

As every student of the Bible will know, the image originated in the *turris eburnea* of the Song of Songs, where it has an entirely different connotation. It is just one item in the long list of ecstatic imagery which the kingly poet devoted to the bodily perfections of his beloved, saying 'Thy neck is as a tower of ivory.'

According to the sources accessible to me, the metaphor appears again in the writings of the French author Charles Augustin St Beuve, in 1831. Although it seems unlikely to me that it should not have been used in earlier literature, it may well be that St Beuve was the first to give it the now familiar connotation. In speaking of the stand taken by the two French poets, Victor Hugo and Alfred de Vigny, during the revolution of 1830, he says: 'Hugo, strong partisan, fought in armour, and held high his banner in the midst of tumult; he still holds it; and Vigny, more discreet, as if in his tower of ivory, retired before noon.'

Here we have the important motive of the artist's retiring from the reality of life. He withdraws into the solitude of the ivory tower, because he loathes the turmoil prevailing elsewhere. His is the attitude of an intellectual aristocrat.

Now we have it on high authority that we are making over our own time into an era to be known as 'the century of the common man', and we are invited to look upon that process as a highly desirable consummation. In point of fact, I do not know whether there is much left to be done in order to achieve this result, as it seems to me that the common man already has been ruling supreme for quite some time. The common man, of course, is just as ill-defined an entity as any of the concepts used freely in political discussion. Incidentally, watching political discussion, one frequently can not help suspecting that concepts in general are practicable for it only as long as they remain ill-defined, but that is here beside the point.

What anybody thinks of the common man depends very largely on whether he wants to be one himself or whether he prefers to be an uncommon man. It has been said that God must have loved the common people because He made so many of them. A different opinion was expressed recently by an American writer, to the effect, that God does not seem to have particularly loved the common people, or else He would not have made them so common. Amusing as it is, this quip may be found a little flippant. Yet, it contains a wholesome revolt against the all-too-readily accepted assumption that everything that appears in overwhelming quantity is sanctified by its multitude.

We are told that the common man is the backbone, prerequisite and result of democracy, and that ought to be enough to make him a sacred cow. Actually I think that the common man is not so much the indispensable material of democracy as the result of industrial mass production. According to what we can gather from advertisements, the ideal conditions of society would be reached if everybody would buy everything. The present calamity which is responsible for certain things not being produced in sufficient quantities is clearly felt as a temporary delay of the forthcoming progress, for even now we are constantly encouraged to save money for the future super-radios, super-washing machines and super-jukeboxes being prepared for us by tireless inventors when they take time off from the more vital affairs of death. Naturally standardised commodities can be sold more smoothly if the prospective customers are standardised, too. In order to make him feel good about being standardised, the common man is being glorified as the true hero of our age. If to be like everybody else is publicised as a special virtue, everybody will be happy to be like everybody else, and business will supposedly flourish, because everybody will be buying what everybody else is buying.

The artist, sitting up in his ivory tower late at night and contemplating the state of this world, finds it not good. One of the outstanding properties of the true art object is its uniqueness, that is, it can not be repeated. The perfect replica of an art object has artistically no value whatever. A copy of the Ninth Symphony by Beethoven is not a second Ninth Symphony, but a copy of the first and only one. With modern production methods countless copies of any art object can be made rapidly and cheaply. Music can be printed in incredible amounts, a performance of music can be made audible to innumerable people through the radio, even long time after the actual playing is over, by means of recording. In this respect the unique work of art enters the process of mass production with a vengeance and becomes subject to its laws. According to strict business standards, the manufacture of new symphonies, for instance, can be justified only, if the old ones are worn out beyond repair and if the new ones can be made faster and cheaper and sold to more people than the old ones, and publishers, makers of records, managers of broadcasts and other commercial administrators of art are forming their policies in precisely these terms. Of course, none of the conditions just mentioned obtains to an appreciable extent, and therefore the making of new symphonies remains an activity largely dedicated to those who are striving at becoming uncommon men. Once upon a time this was considered a natural and highly desirable attitude on the part of everybody. Nowadays we are liable to hear the objection, 'Why, if everybody would become uncommon, there would be no difference, since they would be again all alike.' The fallacy of the argument lies in the tacit assumption that everything, even being outstanding, is, or ought to be, available to everybody. Napoleon is reported to have ascribed the superior quality of his armies to the fact that each soldier, figuratively speaking, had a marshal's baton in his kit. He certainly did not mean to say that all of them could, or would, become field marshals. But he seemed to think that they were so perfect infantry men because each of them was eager to do better than that.

Far be it from me to intimate that worthy intellectual attainments, like for instance, the understanding and enjoyment of art, are accessible to unusually talented and especially trained persons only. What I want to say is that if the abode of the artist appears solitary, aristocratic, and precious and frail, it does so because most people are contenting themselves with undeservedly miserable intellectual habitations, although they could live in a state of comparative luxury if they would decide to make proper use of the faculties granted to nearly all of them by their creator.

I wish I had time to read to you the whole first chapter of a recently published brilliant book, *Education for Freedom* by President Hutchins of Chicago University. Among many amusing, fascinating and challenging things he says this: 'It is obvious that if we succeeded in teaching everybody to read, and everybody read nothing but pulp magazines, obscene literature and *Mein Kampf*, the last state of the nation would be worse than the first. Literacy is not enough. The common answer is that the great books are too difficult for the modern pupil. All I can say is that it is amazing how the number of too difficult books has increased in recent years. The books that are now too difficult for candidates for the doctorate were the regular fare of grammar-school boys in the Middle Ages and the Renaissance. Most of the great books of the world were written for ordinary people, not for professors alone.' In other words, it seems that ordinary people in those bygone times did not think of spiritual attainments as an extravagance, but as a highly desirable fixture of their lives. To them, Aristotle was apparently what the ice-box is to our common man. They also did not feel that the artists or philosophers lived in the rarified atmosphere of ivory towers, for those ordinary people who helped erect the Gothic cathedrals, and on Sundays listened to the complex masterpieces of the polyphonic composers, lived in the same spiritual district as the master-builders and musicians. The artists still live in the same quarter, only the place has become deserted, and they found themselves in solitude because they refused to move into the intellectual slums.

It is a well known fact that ever since airplanes have been whizzing from continent to continent like trolley cars, only more frequently and considerably faster, communications between men, common and otherwise, have become increasingly difficult. We are told that the world is shrinking under our very eyes, and the new maps from whose edges whole continents drop down like crushed peanuts demonstrate that we are living practically next door to the Hottentots as well as to the Eskimos. But what good does it do to us or to them, since there is hardly anything worthwhile that we can communicate about even among ourselves? It is no wonder that we are pinning our hopes upon the common man, since the primitive matters within his reach ultimately remain the only common denominator from which some sort of general understanding may be derived. The regions of higher spiritual attainments, religion, philosophy, art, are being left to the specialists who may take care of them if they want to. Those, however, who are devoted to the spiritual goods with honesty and self-denial are blamed for idling in those ivory towers which seem so far away from the province of the common man.

But they only seem so because of the bad conditions of transportation. Actually it is not so far to go to the ivory tower, and one does not need any streamlined airplane to get there. What one needs, is faith, love, time and concentration. I admit that most of them are very scarce, although they are not rationed at all. As to time, conditions seem to have been slightly better in the not too distant past. In speaking of his student days, Mr Hutchins says: 'We had at that time many advantages that have been denied to college students in recent years, but that may be restored to their successors. We had no radios, and for all practical purposes, no automobiles, no movies, and no slick-paper magazines. We had to entertain ourselves. We could not by turning a small knob or paying a small fee get somebody else to do it for us. It never occurred to us that unless we could go somewhere or do something our lives were empty. We had nowhere to go, and no way to get there.'

In this latter respect, the situation recently has undoubtedly improved. Radios and magazines are still going strong. Nevertheless, there is hope that the feeling of emptiness will eventually so increase, that people may again contemplate approaching the ivory tower. They will find that there is nothing to be afraid of. It is a very handsome, elegant edifice, erected by the best architects, well aired, as it is constantly permeated by the thought of the best minds of mankind, bomb-proof and unaffected by blackouts, as it shines in a light that is invisible to the sharks of the air, and the powers of darkness shall not prevail against it. It is quiet, clean, and offers a magnificent view of the lowlands all around it. By no stretch of imagination, I am afraid, would anybody think of Goheen Hall as of an ivory tower, although remarkable improvements have been made, which make it almost look like one of those who knew it before. Anyhow, we are trying to catch some of the spirit, and you are cordially invited to share it with us.

The French writer, Jules de Gaultier, has interpreted the much-worked metaphor in this way: 'The Poet, retired in his Tower of Ivory, isolated . . . from the world of man, resembles, whether he so wishes or not, another solitary figure, the watcher enclosed for months at a time in a lighthouse at the head of a cliff.'

This is exactly how the artist feels. His place is in the watchtower of civilisation, where he looks far out over past and present to the horizon beyond which the future is looming. To his vision he gives tangible, visible, audible shape through the symbols provided by his art and he is anxious to communicate what he is seeing to those who are able and willing to understand his symbols. You who are studying the grammar and syntax of that language of art are called upon to spread its knowledge and thus contribute to bringing to an end the proverbial loneliness of the Ivory Tower.

19

THE COMPOSER AND THE
INTERPRETER

THE very fact that an institute like the present one, with its imposing array of experts in the various branches of music, is devoting its work to the interpretation of music, proves that an awareness exists in regard to problems coming into being when the performer sets out to make audible the music handed over to him by the composer.

In order to understand the nature of those problems, it will be profitable to turn for a few moments toward history. The further back we go in time, the less we observe of the problems besetting nowadays the art of interpretation, until we reach a point at which no problem whatever exists, because there is no difference between composition and interpretation. In the pre-historic days of music, so we have to assume, the art of composing, that is inventing organised musical sound, was one with the act of interpreting this invention, that is emitting the sound by vocal or instrumental means. In modern terms we call this procedure 'improvisation'. For the understanding of our present problems it is necessary to keep in mind that for a very long time in the history of music this procedure has been, consciously or unconsciously, the ideal towards which all musical activities and disciplines were converging. Music was the organised sound which was heard at the moment of the performance. I expect at this point some astonishment at my putting this idea in the past tense—music 'was'. Most people still think that music is what you hear, meaning that all the other activities necessary to produce the performance, including the act of writing down what is to be played, are of a preparatory nature. This is undoubtedly true, for even those musicians who are able to hear a piece of music to some extent inwardly when they look at the score, simply imagine an actual hearing. However, the cause of our problems is the fact that the preparatory act of writing down the music in the course of history has taken on a constantly increasing significance of its own. In short, music has become literature; that is, the written score has meaning, aesthetic value and the full dignity of an art object, no matter whether, or how often, it is made audible, and it retains all those qualities even when it is only sitting on the book-shelves of the library.

I think it will be considered in keeping with the democratic spirit of this college if I take the liberty to disagree with one of the points made by Mr Charlot in his recent lecture on Abstract Art. His discourse seemed to me to imply that music was less fitted to associate itself with timeless matters than painting, because music was taking place in the dimension of time. As one of my students has put it quite philosophically, there seems to have occurred a confusion between the existence and the experience of music. It is true that music when performed is experienced in time. But so is painting, for nobody looks at a picture for centuries, but only for a limited span of time, usually less than it would take him to listen to a sonata or symphony. And just as the painting is still there even when nobody looks at it for any length of time, so is music still existent even if it is not heard. This condition certainly has never been felt by composers to imply the necessity for occupying themselves with ephemeral matters only; on the contrary, they always have thought that their art was particularly adapted to convey timeless thought.

While in olden times the music sheet was merely a mnemonic

aid for the musician who combined in himself the quality of the inventor and the interpreter of the time, things became different as soon as a division of these qualities occurred, a specialisation of functions, because some individuals appeared more fitted for writing music and others more capable of performing it. Still, as long as music was solidly and clearly tied up with circumscribed ecclesiastical and social functions, the composer, no matter how original, personal or even bold in technical innovations he may have been, was still supplying material for a musical manifestation that was expected to follow an established stylistic pattern and virtually could have been taken for an enormously elaborate improvisation on the part of the singers. Actually even counterpoint, according to prevailing views the most rigidly organised form of music, has been improvised by medieval singers, a game known as *Supra Librum Cantare*, when the participants in the exercise were given a cantus firmus, and each of them added a new voice to it, according to the rules which he knew.

However, the process of dissociation, separating the functions of composer and performer, went on and gained special momentum after 1600, when the centre of gravity in music shifted from the set ritual of ecclesiastical services to the free and boundless field of secular thought. From then on the composers increasingly wanted to make their writings expressive of their increasingly personalised ideas as individuals. The details of this evolution belong in the field of general history of music, and a discussion of them would lead much too far in this context. For the rest, these things are more or less well known.

The essential consequence of this process is that now the performer is given a material that is not any longer supposed to sound like his own invention at the moment of the performance, but has meaning and dignity in itself before it becomes audible. The problems involved arise from the fact that the performer, according to his very nature, which I don't have to analyse psychologically in this circle, still strives at making the material sound as if he were creating in the act of performing it, and I wish to go on record here to the effect that he is absolutely right in this aspiration of his.

The composer, even if he acknowledges and respects this state of affairs—which many composers are not ready to do—feels the need of making his own intentions as clear as possible, be it only for practical reasons. In the first place, he can hardly rely on established stylistic conventions any longer, since such conventions gradually disintegrated during the nineteenth century when originality and uniqueness became more and more desirable as principal attributes of the work of art. Furthermore, music is now as a rule being written not for the purpose of one particular performance, but at least theoretically for an unlimited number of performances removed from the control of the composer in both time and space.

Let us see what means are at the disposal of the composer for transmitting his ideas to the interpreter of his works. Obviously these means are almost exclusively graphic signs. The oldest and most elementary of those signs are known as notation, designating originally pitch level and later also time value of the notes to be played or sung. Looking at our present system of notation, it seems so obvious that we are almost at a loss to understand why it took many centuries of long and tortuous detours to evolve that system. Of course, these detours were by no means due to the ignorance or incapability of earlier musicians, but they were very logical in the light of the purposes that notation had to serve in various periods, according to the character of the music, and that is what makes the history of notation a fascinating field of study, by no means limited to purely philological research.

The first thing for which we are nowadays used to look if we want to find out how to perform a piece of music is the tempo, the indication of the speed. Historically, however, this question did not arise until very late. It is easy to assume that medieval ecclesiastical music was meant to be sung in one certain basic speed that everybody knew. Yet it would be wrong to believe that no variations of that speed were used. Willi Apel, in his book on the history of notation, has brilliantly and in my opinion convincingly pointed out that the so-called proportional system, which was dispensed with by so many earlier musicologists as one of the craziest bubbles produced by scholastic brains, actually served the purpose of indicating variations of speed. According to the tenets of the period these variations were expressed in terms of proportions referring to the all-pervading basic speed. The artistic and intellectual boldness of some of the medievalists went far enough to make them use such fantastic directions as, for instance, that in one voice of the contrapuntal fabric after a certain point thirteen units should cover the same time span as did nine units before that point. Taking into consideration that the other voices would still proceed in the old speed, rhythmic combinations would result of a subtlety and complication that makes the dreaded rhythmic complexity of modern music appear fairly simple. It indicates an entirely different and by no means inferior way of musical thinking.

The modern equivalent of the proportional system is the metronome, by which the varying individual speeds of the music are expressed in relation to the abstract unit of one minute. In the eyes of the composer this should be a great improvement over the vague descriptive indications like Allegro, Andante, and the like. For reasons to be discussed later, the improvement brought on by the metronome is not so unequivocal as one may think.

Another objective of graphic indications approached by the composers still later and with increasing solicitude is dynamics. Not only does the notation in itself not suffice any longer to suggest to the performer what should be loud and what soft, but also the meaning of the music increasingly depends on a very accurate distribution of dynamic shadings. This purpose is achieved by a great number of symbols known as expression marks, which in the romantic period were more and more supplemented by descriptive adjectives, adverbs and whole sentences aiming at conveying extra-musical associations of a poetic nature which the composer wanted to evoke in the performer and eventually in the listener. This procedure implies a fair amount of confidence in regard to a generally shared pattern of emotional reactions and to the automatism of psychological processes. If the composer indicates that a certain phrase is to be played 'with determination' and another 'with tenderness', no technical directions as to the manner of playing are involved. But he hopes that the player, if he generates in himself the attitude of determination or tenderness, will hit upon the technical means necessary for the desired effect. I shall speak later of still another type of graphic signs that the composers use in order to clarify their intentions. This refers to phrasing and articulation.

If this is as far as the composer may go in establishing a text as clear as possible, let us now see how far the interpreter may go in making this text appear his own creation, or nearly so, at the moment of the performance. It will be easy to dispense with the extreme cases in which the performer does not shrink from arranging or paraphrasing the given text by putting in features which would allow him to indulge in mannerisms in which he knows himself to be particularly successful. That may reach from the naïve habit of dwelling unduly on high notes on the part of certain singers to actually writing down special versions, concert arrangements and paraphrases of the given material such as have been left by Franz Liszt and other virtuosos. The more elaborate such arrangements become, the more they take on the character of compositions in their own right and become in turn objects of interpretation. I don't wish to go into the problem as to whether such manipulations should be condemned under all circumstances, or whether they may be justified in some cases. It is well known that in the nineteenth century in general few inhibitions were felt in this respect, and nowadays we shudder at the thought that, for instance, Bach scores were amplified with clarinets and trombones. However, we don't feel any such misgivings playing the Well-Tempered Clavichord on the modern piano, in spite of the tremendous difference between that instrument and Bach's harpsichord.

While one may readily admit that the listeners to the romantic arrangements of Bach's music received a picture far remote from that which the original score conveys, we must also admit that Bach's music has successfully survived any kind of manhandling inflicted upon it, including the swing arrangements which caused such a fuss a few years ago, and if for nineteenth century audiences the only possibility of hearing Bach was to receive him through the medium of the taste of the period, it was perhaps better than nothing at all. It seems plausible enough that each period perceives the art of ages past in the light of its own aesthetic tenets, and the honest efforts made in our own time to get as closely as possible at the originals may involve as great a number of errors as the innocent enthusiasts of the romantic school committed, who, as far as they were honest, were just as convinced as we are that they did their best to serve the true intentions of the great masters.

We may at this point break up the discussion of these affairs, for they transcend the field of what we wish to consider here under the heading of interpretation: that is, the actual rendition of music previously written. In other words we shall confine ourselves to analysing the problems of the interpreter who wants to carry out faithfully the instructions given to him by the composer through the system of the graphic symbols discussed before. As a reaction against the era of the virtuoso who used to manipulate the compositions coming under his hands according to his fancies, we have now established the ideal of work-fidelity; that is, we consciously try to carry out the wishes of the composer. That seems to be simple enough a proposition, since apparently we have just to obey the graphic signs employed by the composer, and at this point I wish to narrow down still further the scope of this discussion by focussing on those cases in which the composer to the best of his knowledge has put down all the indications that seem to him to be necessary in order to insure the proper rendition of his work. In general this will apply to contemporary music, as most composers today are aware of the problems which we are discussing here, so that ultimately we will examine the relationship of the living composer and his contemporary performer.

It will soon appear that the advice just to obey the directions put down in the score does not solve all the problems. A comparison with dramatic literature will elucidate the point. Take the following lines from Hamlet's monologue:

'To die: to sleep
No more; and by a sleep to say we end
The heart-ache and the thousand natural shocks
That flesh is heir to, 'tis a consummation
Devoutly to be wish'd. To die, to sleep;
To sleep: perchance to dream: ay, there's the rub . . .'

Obviously there are a hundred ways of speaking these lines, as far as pitch level, distribution of accents, speed, number and length of breaks are concerned. The repetition of 'To die, to sleep,' and the immediate repetition of the second 'to sleep' clearly require some special treatment in regard to expressive nuances, and doubtless many different possibilities could be chosen and defended. If we would demand that of all these possibilities the one and only should be chosen which Shakespeare had in mind, we would be quite at a loss to decide which one it was. Shakespeare does not give the slightest stage directions as to the mood succession of the monologue. Our only guiding line is the text itself, the succession of thoughts expressed in the words and the context of the dramatic action, from which we have to draw our conclusions as to the state of mind of Hamlet at this particular point. We may try to get some light through examining why he says 'To die, to sleep' instead of putting the stronger alternative later. When he repeats 'to sleep' for the third time, is the increment of emphasis due to the growing attractiveness of the idea? Or may, on the contrary, some doubt have crept in as to whether sleep would be so desirable after all, so that a slightly interrogative inflection would seem in order? 'To die, to sleep; to sleep—to dream perchance?' To be sure, Shakespeare did not put any question mark there, since that punctuation sign might be much too strong for the subtle nuance suggested by the following 'Ay, there's the rub . . .' by which the idea of sleep is finally discarded. Which one of these alternatives is completely true to Shakespeare? I don't think that any amount of research will give a definite answer.

Returning to music, we face somewhat similar problems. Although a musical score is infinitely more exact than a literary text in regard to the elementary facts of pitch level, rhythm, dynamics and the like, there is still a wide margin left for interpretation.

To speak for a few moments of one of the most elementary factors only, the tempo, we will have to face the fact that even the most accurate manner of indicating it, that is by metronome figures, is not quite unequivocal. In the first place, the ideas of the composer on a certain tempo of his own composition are not at all times absolutely the same. This does not imply that he is muddle-headed or that he is unable to make up his own mind. It only illustrates the elementary fact that a work of art, in spite of its inexorable logic, or rather beyond that logic, has various and varying aspects. I would even go so far as to maintain that the number of possibilities in which a work of art may be interpreted convincingly is an indication of its greatness. Only small and insignificant things have only one aspect, allowing only a single interpretation. Secondly, using the metronome in order to specify the tempo of a composition just written requires an amount of self-denial and insensitivity against noise that only a few hardy individuals can muster. Everybody who has played with, or rather against, a metronome will know that after two or three measures he either gets off the beat, or he has the strange feeling as if he were playing under an anaesthetic, not being quite aware any longer of the music he is trying to perform. Obviously based on this experience was a very wise remark that Beethoven attached to one of his own metronome markings to the effect that it ought to be obeyed strictly only for the opening measure of the piece. I am indebted for this information to my friend, Nikolai Graudan. Thus, if a composer writes a metronome marking like, for example, 'quarter notes equal 96', it means probably that 78 would be far too slow, and 120 much too fast, but according to circumstances 88 might be just as admissible as 102. From my own experience I know that in several cases when interpreters suggested to me a tempo somewhat different from the one I had indicated, I was quite satisfied with their version. It is well known that Wagner after some disappointing experience with interpreters who followed faithfully his metronome markings decided to dispense with that kind of indication altogether. Similar things could be said about the relativity of dynamic directions and so forth. All this points to the fact that even careful indications on the part of the composer leave a substantial margin to the interpreter.

Technically speaking, the filling out of that margin is largely assigned to processes which I like to sum up under the heading of articulation. In the set of definitions which I contributed to the Dictionary of the Arts to be published by the Philosophical Library I offered the following about 'articulation': 'devices of composition aiming at clarity of design; purposeful arrangement of musical elements according to the functions which they have to fulfill in the context, especially with a view to properly balancing their metrical weights; phrase construction.' I believe that this definition applies to the work of the composer as well as to that of the performer, and according to my experience the main problem of interpreting contemporary music lies with articulation. Of course, necessity of articulation is by no means limited to modern music, and the excellence of a performance of old music depends to a great extent on clear and intelligent articulation. However, while classical music by and large remains intelligible even if this point is badly neglected, modern music becomes perfect nonsense if not properly articulated. The reason for this is that the basic facts of the tonal idiom, the standard relationship of chords, are familiar enough to make the elementary structure of such a piece perceivable even if the deeper sense remains hidden. In new music written in an unfamiliar idiom the material itself, the strange chords, unusual progressions, the dissonant intervals and so forth, do not evoke any associations with previously known musical features, so that making any impression at all on the listener depends entirely on the eloquence of the rendition, which is more than mere accuracy.

I am using intentionally the term 'eloquence', because it touches at the sphere of rhetoric. The means by which music becomes articulate are closely related to the linguistic devices that impart to speech the sense-making logical, and expressive shadings. The first requirement here is to discriminate between elements of first importance and such of subordinate significance. Naturally in any good composition every single note is necessary and therefore important, but in any kind of context, be it a combination of simultaneously sounding tones or voices, or a succession of phrases and sections, certain things will have to stand out against certain other things, or else the effect will be muddy and dull. While in homophonic music it is usually easy to discover the leading melodic line, it is not so in a complex fabric of several such lines where the emphasis may shift quickly and frequently from one to the other. The composer may try to indicate the differences in significance by various graphic means, but it will be the performer's task to grasp intelligently the proper shadings of emphasis.

As far as the structure as a whole is concerned, it is just as imperative that the performer be aware of the structural function of the different sections, for it is here that the composer can guide him only in a general manner. Everyone knows that a thematic statement has to be played differently from a transition passage, but the problem is how to tell a statement from a transition. In my opinion the secret of a perfect performance consists in making all the details so lively and variegated that the interest of the listener is attracted by what happens in each moment, and at the same time keeping the continuity of the broader span in evidence. Both tasks are the business of articulation. The performer should act as a guide that takes the listener through a new landscape, inviting him to stop and look around at certain points, enjoying the nearer surroundings, then again to keep going steadily until a new point of special interest is reached, preparing him for the strenuous exertions of a climax, making it clear to him that an area of relaxation will follow, or that the end of the journey is near. All this is written down by the composer, to be sure, but most of these things cannot be expressed through special descriptive symbols; they are embodied in the music itself and must be brought to life by someone who understands the musical process.

I said in the beginning that I thought it was the legitimate desire of the performer to make the music appear as if it were created by him in the act of performing it. This he will achieve only if he re-enacts mentally the work of the composer. Composition consists largely in treating, according to certain principles, material furnished by the creative imagination, that is, it is an action going on in the spheres of both freedom and discipline. These spheres are not neatly separated, that is to say: the invention of the material is not entirely free from assumptions, it always is based on some pre-established selection of basic elements, and the treatment to which the material is subjected according to certain principles is not at all devoid of the element of imagination, for in the first place the principles are the expression of a more inclusive artistic vision, and their application allows for a great number of equally good and aesthetically satisfactory variants. In order to strike the balance between vague and vain virtuoso business and dry and deadly pedantry, the performer ought to put himself in the place of the composer, trying at any given point to reconcile the impulses of his imagination with the principle that he has set up for himself, that is, to obey the prescriptions of the composer as well as he can.

Many composers live under the impression that interpreters are their natural enemies, almost as bad as publishers and critics, and they think that the only remedy of the evil would be if the interpreters would stick more faithfully to the text, and nothing else. In his book *Poetique Musicale*, which is a collection of his Harvard lectures, Igor Stravinsky takes great pains to make this point, admonishing his interpreters to forget all about their own individuality and to obey blindly the directions of the composer. In the case of the highly mechanised type of music that Stravinsky writes and advocates such an attitude on the part of the interpreter may indeed be most conducive to producing an adequate picture of the art object. But in most other cases the composer insisting upon faithfulness to the best would seem to be carrying coals to Newcastle, for contemporary interpreters are anyhow more than intent upon playing what's written on the music sheet, and nothing else. Paradoxically as it seems, I venture to say that if there is any trouble with interpretation, it is mainly due to the fact that interpreters are trying too hard to suppress their own imagination in rendering music. Of course, giving rein to one's imagination is not identical with not paying any attention to the composer's indications. But you remember that I decided to talk on those interpreters who are above the level of neglectful ignorance.

A story was passed around about the great German playwright, George Kaiser, who when he was pestered by a certain stage director with requests to permit him to change one line of Kaiser's play and then another line and still another line finally lost his patience and wired back: 'Change anything you want except title of play and name of author,' for these were the only two things necessary in order to collect royalties for the copyrighted item. I am not suggesting that a composer as a rule should take so cynical an attitude towards what happens to his work, but my own experience has shown me that composers frequently are much more tolerant in regard to interpretation than the interpreters are themselves. Composers who think that there is only one single way of interpreting their music could perhaps derive some hope from new developments in the province of electrical instruments. In my book *Music Here and Now* I outlined an interesting situation in which the acts of composing and interpreting might again coincide in a manner entirely unforeseen. Even in earlier times composers, such as Mozart for instance, wrote pieces for mechanical instruments, but in these cases the composition was written in the usual way on paper, and afterwards transferred onto the mechanical device by engineers. Only in our time a few composers like Hindemith have tried to cut their own rolls for a pianola. Now theoretically it should not be impossible to cut a phonograph record without the music's ever having been played beforehand. However, it seems more than unlikely that a proper mechanical process could ever be devised for producing the necessary grooves accurately. It seems much less unlikely that a contrivance could be invented which would enable a person to design a sound curve onto the light-sensitive film of a sound track. How it could be done, I don't know. It would certainly require infinite study to manage properly all the finesses of such a complete curve in order to get in the full range of tone colours and dynamic shadings that we want to apply in our music. Obviously we would eventually be able to obtain unheard-of tone colours and sound combinations such as could never be arrived at on any of our present instruments. Certainly one could not draw such curves with a clumsy pencil, but perhaps the physicists would present us with a manoeuverable light beam that could leave the desirable traces on the film. The point that seems interesting in the context of this discussion is that the composer would obtain an authentic interpretation by eliminating the interpreter altogether. His act of writing down the music by means of the magical light beam would not produce a set of graphic signs to be read and interpreted by someone else; its result would be the sound-producing device itself. The performance would not contain a single element that was not put there by the composer.

That sounds very interesting and attractive for purists, but the essential question is whether the composer is really interested in such a type of unique and unchangeably set performance, or whether he should be so interested. It is true that the composer is, and ought to be, convinced of the uniqueness of his message, and he naturally is most anxious to get it across to the listeners in undistorted and unadulterated fashion. It is also natural that he might be over-anxious in this respect, seeing that he is practically helpless as soon as he has handed over his music to the interpreter. During the act of the performance in which his message undergoes the supreme test of facing the reaction of those for whom it was destined, the composer is a passive onlooker. However, he should have confidence enough in human nature so as to enjoy rather than to fear the medium of personal life through which his message is filtered before it reaches whom it concerns. The personality of the interpreter is not necessarily a stumbling block on which the work of art goes to pieces, although in only too many unfortunate cases it may be one; in the good cases which ideally should be the rule, that personality vouchsafes an increment of vitality that is not only desirable, but truly necessary in order to put the message across. The interpreter is the first with whom the composition has registered; he, as its first recipient, has had an experience akin to that of the listener, only many times more intense. This enables him to communicate the message to the audience. If composers frequently despair of the possibility of such desirable conditions, it is due to the fact that interpreters of contemporary music more often than not are incapable of fulfilling their assignments. I don't wish to duplicate the efforts of my friends and colleagues who have worked the better part of this summer here to clarify these problems and to suggest remedies for the shortcomings of the art of interpretation. The composer may contribute to the improvement of the situation if he takes the trouble of teaching the interpreters, making them acquainted with the nature and meaning of the creative processes and showing them how a composition originates and of what it is made. I am glad that Black Mountain College has offered me the opportunity of discussing some problems of composition with the young performing artists assembled here, and I hope it has been to their benefit as well as to that of the art that is so close to our hearts.

20

THAT NOISE CALLED MUSIC

RADIO takes the musical work out of its original context. Music was for the most part never intended to be heard in the living-room. The simple but significant result of this change is that music is constantly being heard at a much reduced level of aural volume. Composers of symphonic works may not always have included the size of concert halls and of audiences in their calculations, but they certainly never foresaw that their works would be listened to by an infinite number of individuals, each in his own separate room. If symphonic music exerts any social influence at all, if it is capable of transforming a motley crowd into a community of beings with a more or less similar spiritual outlook, this power is severely handicapped by reduced tonal volume and the isolation of its listeners.

The musician who wishes to concentrate on the quality of a composition or performance naturally welcomes the objectivity inherent in radio reproduction. As long as everything remains in proportion, the reduction of volume does not worry him. He can arrange the lights in his room just as he wishes them to be, can follow the score at will, can smoke, drink or do whatever he thinks necessary to put him into a suitable frame of mind.

Most of our concert halls are, in any case, too large and acoustically of doubtful quality, so that even in those places which appear to be designed for it, the music, coming to the ear from a distant corner, sounds indistinct and distorted. I can think of a very fine-looking concert hall in the Middle West which gives nobody any reason to complain that he is not getting his moneysworth: every note is lovingly echoed three times. And in another hall of my experience, many a symphony sounds like a piece for solo tuba with orchestral interludes: whenever the softest grunt emerges from that towering brass funnel nothing else can be heard. Radio engineers are, as a rule, able to avoid such crudities.

Radio broadcasts therefore, by removing the distractions implicit in a 'live' performance, are an aid to wise and serious concentration. Yet nonetheless several disturbing factors have emerged in the routine of radio presentation. Stuck fast in memories of early stages of their development, radio companies persist in putting music across as if it were a novelty. As many of us can still recall, it was the sense of sharing instantaneously in something happening many miles away that made our first experiences of radio appear so sensational. Since then twenty years have passed, but in the studio the feeling of wonder still lingers. The fact that one can listen to the *Ninth Symphony* at home is considered much less important than the fact that this same *Ninth Symphony* is being played some two thousand miles away. 'We are now taking you to Carnegie Hall', the announcer says, and the illusion of a visit is at once emphasised by the sound of tuning instruments. However, when this procedure is repeated week after week, one begins to suspect that the sound comes from a specially prepared gramophone record: it seems unlikely that every Sunday at exactly the same time the identical tuning noises are to be heard in Carnegie Hall.

In radio circles, reality itself is considered to be less reliable than a concoction of the typical manifestations of reality. One radio manager used to tell, not without an undertone of cynicism, a story of the raw early days of broadcasting. It had been advertised that on Christmas Eve there would be a relay of the great bell of a cathedral. Just before the broadcast was due to begin a cable broke: the damage was irreparable. In the depths of despair the radio company sent for the tympanist of the local opera house. He reached the studio with his instruments in the nick of time. And as he manipulated his cymbals and his gongs the announcer, his voice throbbing with emotion, told of the hallowed bell sending its message out into the Holy Night. Not a single listener noticed that he was being tricked.

Some years ago another radio station went to the other extreme with a 'live' broadcast. A reporter was sent complete with microphone into some swampy forest to pick up the trills of the nightingales who were thought to live there. A rash enterprise, for who could say whether the stars would be willing to co-operate? The main burden fell on the man with the microphone: he and not the nightingale had the job of evoking the magic of that mild May night. Surely it would have been easier to have put on a record of a nightingale singing in the zoo and to have read over it a stunning description of a May night as it should be, penned by a resourceful scriptwriter in the middle of January; or—even better still—to have dropped the whole bag of tricks in favour of a sensible programme.

All this goes to show that events, to be thought worthy of radio presentation, must be pressed into the mould of reporting. When it is music that has to be put over, the process becomes perhaps a bit more complicated. So long as the performance takes place in a studio, things are relatively easy. But even then there is a noticeable tendency to give the impression of a 'live' performance. An imaginary audience is encouraged to inspire the artists by strenuous applause; or the announcer, after dutifully mentioning that the ensuing programme is recorded, will proclaim, 'The artists appearing today are . . .' so as to make us believe that Lily Pons is really there.

One might feel that in a studio concert it would be quite enough just to give the names of the works played and the people playing them. But the announcer takes another view. He presents the music as if it were part of some unique experience occurring in the studio. Musical titbits scattered about in a non-musical programme serve the opposite purpose: they give the factual material a background of fantasy.

Everybody knows that motor manufacturing organisations have a habit of sponsoring entire symphony orchestras together with expensive conductors and soloists. Why do they do it? I am still looking for the man who in the act of buying a car exclaims, 'A Ford of course: no one conducts better than Ormandy!' Nor have I yet heard anybody who, having decided on a Chrysler, has been suddenly smitten by pangs of conscience and has said, 'No, I can't do this to General Motors who put on those splendid Toscanini concerts.' It seems that some of the industrial giants enjoy being associated with artistic greatness. Not that they expect bigger sales from it, but it gives them the appearance of being educators when they get Toscanini to conduct Beethoven.

Music lovers might feel that in matters of this sort more respect was shown in feudal times. They picture the king entering a richly and elegantly decorated Baroque hall, where beautiful ladies and imposing gentlemen are gathered to hear the symphony commissioned by His Majesty: a picture apparently far more in accord with the sublime spirit of music than that of a hard-bargaining, cheque-flourishing publicity agent. Yet quite a few of the kings and bishops who paid for the exquisite musical blossoms of their own day had no higher conception of 'public service' than our modern businessmen. They too sponsored music for the sake of a vaguely defined publicity. If the price we have to pay for an hour of good music is five minutes of attention to a poem about the virtues of rubber tyres and undercarriages, are we any worse off than Mozart's contemporaries, who had to make their bows to the royal box before they could settle down to enjoy the music? And if we cannot conceive what General Motors get from engaging the NBC Orchestra, should we not equally ask ourselves how the lavishness of those Baroque princes repaid itself? It is, of course, possible that some of them loved music. But that possibility is not ruled out among capitalists either. Between the old days and now there is, as far as I can see, only one very great difference: in those times it was fashionable to sponsor contemporary music; today that is certainly not the case.

A sponsor of public performances hopes that people will be led by the pleasure of their experience to think of him, and he is confident that this will eventually bring its reward. It is taken for granted that entertainment leaves behind pleasant impressions. But if entertainment does mean enjoyment, every one who listens to music will want to get enjoyment from it. And opinions differ widely about what constitutes enjoyment. Some people enjoy playing chess, others like smashing lamp-posts.

Since the people who subsidise radio music are manufacturers of articles for mass consumption, they go for works which will give enjoyment to as many listeners as possible. Now the most popular form of enjoyment is, without a doubt, love. The musical experience of the 'ordinary man' is frequently connected with affairs of the heart: he takes his girl friend to a dance for instance, thus paving the way for a less formal approach. So it is felt that the music which serves such ends must possess an absolute enjoyment value. And for that reason, the radio with devastating logicality pumps out dance music at all times of day. In consequence the state of bliss engendered by music becomes associated irrevocably with the idea of the noisy consumption of expensive drinks.

Disgruntled highbrows are brushed aside with the excuse that this is exactly what the majority wants, and it is not only expedient but also democratic to provide it. Unfortunate, but very true. Complex characters who, though not immune to the joys of love or even of cocktail bars, have a wider conception of 'enjoyment', are free to switch off and await those problematic broadcast programmes which the industrial tycoons project.

But the purveyors of dance music are mistaken if they imagine that highbrows have no time at all for their wares. In fact, there is scarcely one among the hundreds of serious musicians I have known who does not find some enjoyment in jazz. Most of them, I suspect, have found even more enjoyment in it than the 'ordinary man' for the reason that they know more about the way it works: their enjoyment is based on informed judgment. It is certainly both possible and indeed desirable to take pleasure equally in the *Eroica* and in *Caldonia*. Everything in its proper time and place.

Radio, which supplies both sorts, is not organised to sharpen critical wits into the bargain. That, and not the prejudiced attitude of the highbrows, is the real trouble.

Throughout the day the radio set delivers its acoustic stimulants with no discernible shades of contrast. We are taken at one time to the tabernacle at Salt Lake City, at another to the centre of Chicago's night life, now to the 'Palladium' of Hollywood, at other times to the Carnegie Hall or into a studio or a cathedral or a fairground. And it all sounds exactly the same, rather mushy, rather treacly, an unceasing ghostly gloss, diminished as a rule to form a tolerable background noise for the accomplishment of household tasks. The average listener (the one who makes a habit of keeping his set switched permanently on) is never given any hint that it might be worth his while to readjust his listening apparatus when a Beethoven symphony is being played. All that in the nature of things he is aware of on such occasions, is that the background noise has assumed a somewhat unusual flavour, and if the strangeness is pushed beyond a certain point he will, thrown off his mental balance, put an abrupt end to the spectre.

This climatic moment, more feared by radio people than damnation itself, is reached most frequently when new music is put on the air. Though Beethoven and Schubert may have nothing to do with jazz, one tends to accept the vocabulary they use as a harmless prototype of later discoveries. A listener who is used to the simple structure and the strong stimulants of jazz music will probably be bored by passages in classical works in which relatively simple sound patterns are marked by all the greater intensity of expression. But he will only be bored, whereas contemporary music with its hard sounds, jagged contours, startling turns and its many complex relationships, really antagonises him. It contains nothing that 'gets' him. Accessibility is, however, the most important component of that animal sense of well-being which the big boys of radio are out to convey. Music, whose job it is to beautify our homes like a sort of acoustical wallpaper, must be music that is familiar to everyone or at any rate sounds familiar. Revelations, confessions, problems—manifestations of struggle and defeat—would ruin the wallpaper.

The music that is put out on the radio nowadays gets swallowed up in effect in a thick fog of noise from which only trumpet players, bandleaders, virtuoso conductors and wailing heartthrob experts, trained in the art of putting themselves across, emerge: the friendly household gods of the 'ordinary man', putting in their appearance at set hours. They go along together with those other Lares and Penates of modern man, the heroes of the comic strips. The housewife is soon held in thrall to the friendly spirit, and she becomes a fan: a Sinatra fan, a Toscanini fan or whatever it may be. Yet I have never heard of any lady who through the medium of radio has become a Beethoven fan. Not even Brahms (who for some unexplained reason is the only serious composer permitted to measure his strength against the ubiquitous Russians) is as familiar to listeners as any of the stick-waggers who keep the musical tapeworm going.

Who can say exactly what this unending stream of radio music has done to the millions of people who are subjected to it? Yet one thing should at any rate have become clear by now: the idea that by pumping masses of music into their homes, people are transformed into connoisseurs, is a mistaken one.

Whatever music might do, it does only when one approaches it with an open heart and shares actively in its being. All these millions have been absorbing music in a way that is highly dangerous: they simply cannot live without a habitual background noise. Perhaps they will have developed a superficial sense of discrimination. Whoever stares for years at the wallpaper in his room is bound one day to notice that the second leaf of the seventh rose to the left of the wardrobe is darker than the other leaves, but he will still know nothing at all about the art of painting.

Of course there is always the chance that a few of those who have ears to hear will be affected (though they will certainly have to use some other means than radio to get their ears in training). And perhaps that rumoured innkeeper out in the wilds who but for radio would never have discovered the glories of symphonic music does really exist somewhere. Nevertheless the question remains whether such a result justifies the enormous waste and the terrifying drop in values inherent in such musical inflation.

There are some hypocrites about who have spread the idea that by jazzing up the classics one can bring 'good music to the masses'. However, no one has yet succeeded in demonstrating that a person ignorant of classical music has been won over to Mozart through hearing those eight bars of the C Major piano sonata which tinkle through a popular swing number bearing the classical title 'In an Eighteenth Century Drawing Room'. Still, daylight robbery of this sort is not worth the indignation which it has aroused among self-appointed guardians of the Grail. It is true that Botticelli's Venus should not be made to serve as a pin-up girl; but if it is, the painting remains what it always was. The delicate and subtle music of Mozart is made of sterner stuff than those who have abused it: many masterpieces have survived long periods of silence in which scarcely an ear was turned towards them; they will also survive the period in which far too many ears are turned to them far too often and far too idly.

What happens to music on its way through the ether confirms the opinion held by some that mankind lets its power of invention run away with it. We are dissipating our musical heritage for the sake of one ingenious machine and are heading for a musical famine. True progress will be possible only when listeners alter their ideas about what they expect from music. But it is unlikely that the radio will make them do that.

21

WHY 'PALLAS ATHENE WEEPS'

SINCE my schooldays, classical Greece has constantly fascinated and occupied me. As far as I can recall, this interest always
sprang from my belief that I could see connections between the
events of classical antiquity and the problems of today. In an
essay on the pre-history of *Pallas Athene Weint* I have described
how, while still at school, I tried to make the exciting figure of
Alcibiades the subject of a novel (luckily I never finished it)
which translated the fantastic adventures of the arch-rogue into
modern terms. And I produced other literary efforts on classical
themes, with similar aims.

My next encounter with Greek antiquity occurred after I had
realised that by nature I was really fitted to approach the substance of human life through the medium of music. In 1923 I
turned Oskar Kokoschka's play *Orpheus und Eurydike* into an
opera. At that time I was really far from clear as to what
Kokoschka had seen in the ancient myth, but today I think I
appreciate better what attracted me so much to his version.
Although he did not put the characters into modern dress, he
gave the myth an interpretation that only a completely modern,
psychological mind could have reached. What fascinated me
and inspired me to interpret the drama musically was that I
realised, in a flash, that a basically simple story, whose logic
seemed to depend on forgotten promises, could suddenly be
seen in quite a different light, without losing its emotional logic.

Six years later I turned to another subject from Greek
mythology, which I myself put into the dramatic shape I

wanted. While Greece, as a geographical concept, plays virtually no part in *Orpheus und Eurydike*, the physical and mental climate of Greece are of central significance in *Das Leben des Orest*. In *Jonny Spielt Auf* I had already tried to make the geographical opposition between East and West, Europe and America, a symbol of the dramatic tension of the subject. In *Das Leben des Orest* the axis on which the dramatic action turns runs north-south. The sensuous directness of the Greek nature is contrasted with the brooding abstraction of northern Tauris.

While these geographical features of the legend are strongly emphasised, its remoteness in time is deliberately played down. The mythical timelessness of the events is brought out by the fact that motivations are often given them which belong to the stock of experience of our own time. The supernatural elements of the myth are left untouched, as a dynamic force that promotes the action, but I have often given them another, rational interpretation drawn from modern psychological thinking. Pallas Athene, who causes Orestes to be freed by casting her divine vote in the court verdict and so proclaiming a new legal order, is not presented as a *dea ex machina:* the miracle has long been prepared rationally. But that does not make it any less of a miracle than if the goddess took a hand personally.

Contemporary ideas show particularly clearly in the politico-social side of the drama. This may seem surprising on the stage, particularly if the production stresses it, but in reality it is fairly obvious. Even if the expressive forms of social life are subject to striking changes throughout history, the effective impulses within them remain essentially the same. If, in portraying something which moves us, a work of art wants to get critical distance, it is more likely to convince and endure if it presents this generally moving subject in a remote period of time.

In *Pallas Athene Weint*, the problems of man's social life play an important part. But the reciprocal action—the collective influences the individual and stimulates impulses in him that reflect back on the collective—bring the individual back into the foreground which he must always occupy in drama, and particularly in opera.

The figure of Pallas Athene is the only mythical element that stretches across from the world of Orestes to the world of modern opera. Apart from her, the opera is founded on what is called—more confidently than convincingly—historical reality. The legendary freeing of Orestes symbolised the transition from a way of life expressed by blood-lust, truce-oaths and revenge to an order founded on rational humanity and individual freedom. As a model and home of this, as it were, Apolline order, the goddess founded Athens. The Dionysian, dark side of human nature was neither belied nor suppressed. It produced the Eleusine mysteries which allow for the darker irrational impulses. The ideal Athens was aiming at, in the opinion of those who understand the purpose of the divine founder, is a delicate and vigorous balance of all the innumerable and often conflicting impulses whose political framework is described by the very elastic term 'democracy'.

Socrates is portrayed as one of those sages who represent an ideal of human dignity that allows them to live in such a way that they do not need to injure either themselves or any other power. As we know, Socrates paid for possessing this human dignity with his life. Three of his pupils show how his teaching founders when it is made to stand the test of a political crisis in the public actions of these men: Alcibiades, to whom humanity means ruthlessly living one's own life to the full, destroys Athens; Meton, who is determined to follow Socrates' teaching fanatically, carries it *ad absurdum*, and Meletos betrays both the teaching and the master.

The political crisis is the Peloponnesian War in which Athens has to defend her shifting social balance against the attack of a monolithic power. The actual content of the Spartan state-doctrine is deliberately not defined more precisely, The fact that its practitioners consider it unchangeable and absolutely valid shows clearly enough that it is the very opposite of the Athenian doctrine. 'We have seen the light. We know what we and all humanity need,' says Agis, King of Sparta, and this drives him to try and stamp out a type of state which rejects such ambitions.

The thing that sets the dramatic action in motion is the mutilation of the sacred statue of Hermes in Athens on the eve of the Sicilian expedition in which the Athenians hope, in a final effort, to push back their opponents' front line with a formidable flanking movement. Alcibiades, who has just been chosen to lead the expedition, is suspected of the outrage. An unscrupulous sensualist, he has already been guilty of several offences against the good old customs of the Republic, and this crime too is ascribed to him.

Meletos, another pupil of Socrates, has counselled riskier and riskier military policy in the name of the hereditary freedoms of Athens; on the other hand he envies Alcibiades for his dazzling, devil-may-care character. He seems inclined to suspect Alcibiades but gives this up when it emerges that he is so popular with the navy that it would refuse to sail if its admiral were recalled and arraigned.

The third pupil, Meton, is a radical pacifist who tries to incite the crowd to rebel against the campaign because he believes that if the Athenian ideal is peace, they should simply stop waging war. Socrates saves Meton from the bellicose mob and raises the awkward question of how they propose to justify forcing Meton into silence in the name of the freedom they want to defend.

The suspicion against Alcibiades becomes all the more palpable when a rumour gets abroad that he has profaned the

Eleusine mysteries. Althaea, the priestess of Eleusis, calls him to account. She is sure it was he who got into the temple in disguise during one of their secret ceremonies and tried to insult her. Even though she objected to this out of religious conviction she still fell into the power of this irresistible seducer and now feels bound to him, in some mystic way, for ever. Although Alcibiades neither denies nor admits this, he indicates that he would not be disinclined to do what Althaea accuses him of.

While Alcibiades is making good strategic progress in Sicily his opponents prevail in Athens and get him recalled. He pretends to obey the order but escapes from the ship bringing him back, goes to Sparta and gives away Athens' plans, which eventually leads to the downfall of the Athenian navy and army in Sicily. As the opportunity offers, he does not even stick at making the Queen of Sparta his mistress.

Up to this point the broad lines of the action are historically documented, even if the events are rather compressed in time. Thucydides writes in detail about the preparation for the Sicilian expedition and the destruction of Hermes. I brought out Meletos' role more strongly because later he was to oppose Socrates and bring a charge against him. Plutarch recounts Alcibiades' escapades and mentions the profanation of the mysteries without going into details. The character of Althaea and her relationship to Alcibiades are freely invented. But Plutarch mentions a Meton who, to escape war-service, first set fire to his house and then pleaded before the authorities that a man so injured could not be drafted. Alcibiades' treachery and seduction of the Queen of Sparta are also documented.

The famous trial of Socrates has been described in detail. But, as I found, certain historians have expressed the view that the indictment, as it has been handed down to us, hardly justifies the procedure of the prosecutors and judges; they have surmised that the trial might have been based on evidence that was not allowed to come out in the proceedings for political reasons. Taking a hint from this, I constructed Meletos' plot to destroy the Hermes so as to discredit Alcibiades. In this plot he makes use of Meton, the pacifist, who is only too glad to join in because he hopes the crime will mean that the Sicilian campaign will be called off. As the plot fails and the campaign takes place, Meton hides himself in the caves in the Hymettos mountains. Socrates finds him there and appeals to his conscience. Meton's obstinate, Timon-like attitude collapses and he lets Socrates into the secret. From then onwards Meletos risks everything to stop Socrates talking. When the Spartans occupy Athens, Meletos, who has long since converted Athenian democracy into a police state on the pretext of defending liberty, speedily and easily moves into a position of trust in the new autocratic regime. As it needs a scapegoat to win over the masses, Meletos proposes Socrates, and should Socrates divulge the secret, he is prepared to undermine his credit by a large-scale popular accusation.

This part of my drama is poetic licence. In reality there were many years between Alcibiades' treachery and the final defeat of Athens. In consequence of his affair with the Queen of Sparta, he thought it more prudent to withdraw first into neutral Persia. From there he once again established relations with the Athenians and produced a few more military successes for them. Nevertheless Athens never managed to recover completely from the Sicilian catastrophe. In the end Alcibiades was killed by the brothers of a woman he had seduced; they set fire to the house in which he was living with her and, having smoked him out, killed him with their spears when he tried to escape. I copied this situation, externally at least, by making the relentless Althaea her seducer's nemesis.

The Athenian democracy collapses because it is so fascinated by the scintillating personality of its best military defender,

200

Alcibiades, that it attaches no importance to his ethical irresponsibility, and partly because its political adviser, Meletos, can think of no other treatment for what he assumes is the weakness of democracy than gradually to make it so like its 'monolithic' enemy that the war becomes meaningless. The result is that the end could hardly have been worse if Athens had followed Meton, who was against fighting from the very beginning.

By rejecting Meletos' hypocritical offer to let him escape from prison after the trial, Socrates assumes the responsibility, theoretically, for the catastrophe. He is to suffer for the fact that the Athenians have not acted up better to his teachings. But perhaps his real guilt is that in assuming this responsibility he forces his compatriots to be guilty of killing an innocent man. But within this two-fold tangle the two protagonists, Socrates and Athens, kindle a warning beacon in world history and point the way to final atonement, even if it is still very remote. The hellish shrieks with which the exterminators thought they would seal the end of Athens become the great song of lamentation with which Pallas Athene transfigures it. Our greatest hope is that a god may weep for us.

22

THE LIBRETTO PROBLEM

'LET them hear the words!' Many an opera conductor has crossly shouted that up to the stage when he noticed in rehearsal that the singers were reducing the libretto to such incomprehensible gibberish that spectators would be forced to buy a copy of the text if they were to understand what was going on.

The trouble stems from the fact that the nature and training of most singers predispose them to consider the text as a matter of minor importance. Of course they know that they are there to present human characters on the stage and that these characters are defined not only by the music the composer has provided but by the words in the libretto. But the tradition of sensuality in singing lays the principal stress on beautiful tone, and it not infrequently happens that the singer feels that not only the words but even the music get in his way when he is trying to deliver the goods. A man with no feeling for music would hardly think of becoming a violin virtuoso merely because he happened to have inherited a splendid violin; for even if in some way he could acquire the necessary skill to draw sweet sounds from the instrument, he still would not be able to present musical ideas. But there are many singers who follow that profession simply because nature has endowed them with useful vocal chords (even though it has denied them musical intelligence). And singing teachers rarely make any effort to compensate for this lack, partly because they are not capable of it and partly because the connection between music and singing has never occurred to them. But even intelligent, musical singers tend to look to the tone and let the words go by the board in the heat of the battle. It is at moments like these that the conscientious conductor will step in—even if people often object that his exhortations will have no effect, because you can never hear the words of an opera, and what is more it is not necessary because in any 'real' opera the words are of no consequence in any case.

Experience has shown that the first argument is just not true. If the singers have the necessary technical instruction and constant, tireless guidance from the conductor, most of the words of most operas can be understood perfectly well—given, that is, a theatre of reasonable proportions and moderately favourable acoustical properties. One does not need to be a specialist on the subject to see that comprehensibility depends mainly on articulating the consonants clearly and that it is precisely the consonants that singers try to minimise, because one cannot produce beautiful tone on them.

The other enemy of the text is the orchestra. With composers such as Monteverdi, Handel, Mozart, Verdi, Puccini and in fact most of the earlier opera writers, this is no problem, because the orchestra is usually moderate in size and treated in such a way that the voices always dominate. The difficulties begin with Wagner, who enriched the opera orchestra with heavy, thick textures and gave it its much-vaunted symphonic independence. But even in Wagner the words can be made surprisingly comprehensible if the conductor does not let himself be carried away by the orchestral torrent in which the voices will drown, like Valhalla in the Rhine. But there are wide tracts of Strauss where one can only give up in despair—particularly in works such as *Der Rosenkavalier*, where there is a great deal of everyday conversational style to be got across—for Strauss's orchestra is often even larger and more 'independent' than Wagner's. This seems to support the second argument that words are not important, for *Der Rosenkavalier* is in fact one of the most successful operas of the century. Obviously the public will put up with not understanding the words. And yet this libretto, like nearly all those Strauss set, is of a high literary standard, unlike the libretti of older operas from which the argument derives—although it is in these operas that one can nearly always understand the words very well.

Since the twenties the 'problem of opera' has remained an inexhaustible subject of discussion. Above all, of course, the problem is that contemporary operas (with certain exceptions) no longer have the ready or enthusiastic, and at any rate, constant reception accorded to older works firmly rooted in the repertory. When the rebuilt Vienna Opera House was opened an authoritative voice suggested the explanation that present-day composers ask too much of opera intellectually. They have too much respect for the medium, it was said, and this is why they load up their efforts with much too demanding intellectual cargo, completely forgetting that intellectually the opera public is no more elevated than the football-watching public.

Nobody can really verify this last statement. At least it is true that, since Wagner gave the musical theatre 'cosmic' significance in the most palpable way, the significance-potential of opera can no longer be ignored. Whether the composer tries to realise it or expressly rejects it, some kind of intellectual statement will always be expected from a new opera of any calibre—something more than the sentimental affairs of fictional characters or a pleasing arrangement of vocal fireworks. Even the football crowd in the stalls expects it, without confessing the fact. For a trivial new work bores them even more than a more demanding one. They may enjoy *La Bohème*, but if a new *Bohème* could be written today they would not find it particularly interesting.

But the question arises as to whether the old opera libretti, damned as 'silly' and inferior literature, but at the same time praised for being so 'light' intellectually, were really so naïve and guileless. This can hardly be said of one of the very earliest libretti, on which one of the greatest of all operas is built. In Monteverdi's *Incoronazione di Poppaea* Seneca, who indulges in general precepts, is a central figure in the drama, and one of the most exciting scenes consists of a long politico-philosophical dialogue between the sage and his pupil Nero, led astray into cynicism by Poppaea. You may object that this opera has not 'lasted'. But this needs qualification. True, *Poppaea* has not been played constantly in every opera-house from Aachen to Zagreb, but latterly hardly a year has passed when this master-piece, newly edited by great musicians of our age, has not been both produced and discussed. There is a kind of vitality which cannot be measured by box-office receipts.

But indeed even operas as 'successful' as Mozart's are by no means without elements deliberately designed to make the spectator think—whether it is done elegantly, wittily, as in *Figaro* and *Cosi*, or with the naïveté of *The Magic Flute*, which can only be enjoyed today with a great effort of good will. A similar primitive style and indescribable clumsiness get in the way of *Fidelio's* message, but there can be no doubt as to the seriousness of Beethoven's intentions. Meyerbeer is the first to give the opposite impression: one feels that the bitter theme of religious war meant no more to the composer of *Les Huguenots* and *Le Prophète* than a pretext for overblown costume drama. And for this very reason his operas strike us as flat and stale today, despite the often attractive verve and masterly stagecraft of the music. I would like to bet that Gounod's *Faust* has not escaped this fate because its music is so much better than Meyerbeer's—in fact the reverse is not hard to demonstrate—but because, despite his earnest efforts, the composer did not succeed in de-Goethe-ising the subject completely and reducing it to triviality.

In comparison with these works, modern opera reveals its intellectual side much more clearly. And it is one of the strange, dialectical tricks of history that the intellectual element has been pushed forward so much just because people wanted to get away from Richard Wagner, who had given it the foremost place in music-drama. The message Wagner wanted to convey was to be made irresistible by the enchantment of the total work of art, the magic fusion of all the arts. Of them all, music was supposed to exert the strongest hypnotic power. The psychological medium of the undertaking was the creation of total illusion. The spectator was no longer merely to enjoy seeing dressed-up men and women hoodwinking each other, as in the old operas, but to be so overpowered by the whole integrated spectacle as to believe in a kind of temporary reincarnation of the gods and heroes. Making the orchestra invisible was one of the means to this end.

Those who reacted against this ecstatic concept of opera emphasised both its artificial and its intellectual elements, in varying degrees. On the one side there are the grandiosely artificial solutions such as Stravinsky's *Oedipus Rex*, on the other the efforts to expose the artificiality of the theatre, such as the 'epic' drama of Brecht and Weill and the large-scale projects such as Milhaud's *Christophe Colomb* and my own *Karl V*. In these the drama is both presented and discussed, and the music, in which the tension between the reality of the discussion and the unreality of the so-called 'action' is discharged, is there to give a basis for the co-existence of the two spheres. What all these interpretations of musical drama have in common is their critical attitude towards the idea, which Wagner started, of its being a magic self-contained world.

It is all the more natural for modern opera-librettists to for-

207

mulate ideas since they generally prefer prose to verse. This is due to the fact that modern music tends away from symmetrical period structure and goes in for freely articulated phrases with the accents distributed irregularly. It is interesting that Mozart, whose musical thinking follows tradition in aiming at symmetrical period structure, considered verse indispensable, but rhyme a disadvantage. If lines that scan regularly are considered useful for producing similarly regular musical forms, there can be no objective objection to rhyme, for it certainly does not make the lines any less regular than they would be without it. Mozart did not oppose rhyme for musical reasons, but because he thought librettists tended to sacrifice the meaning to the rhyme—another proof of how much the thought-content of their libretti mattered even to such completely 'musical' opera composers as Mozart.

The idea that a prose libretto is an advantage to an opera has, no doubt, been fostered by the fact that an ever-increasing number of composers decide to write their own libretti. Once again, Wagner is responsible for the present-day feeling that a libretto should have literary merit in its own right. From Busenello, who wrote *Poppaea*, to Illica and Giacosa, who supplied Puccini, librettists were not such literary barbarians as people are inclined to assume, although they would probably have been the last to recommend their creations as works to be read. Their task was essentially to ravel and unravel the dramatic situations which were to inspire the composer's creative gifts in such a way that the dimensions demanded by a well-founded convention worked out appropriately; and to provide the lyrical oases necessary for the arias with the obvious dolor-onor, Liebe-Triebe, heart-part rhymes. Wagner, who felt the need to express something more than these primitive 'ideas' in his music-dramas, invented his own language, which is undoubtedly original, even if its literary merit is questionable.

Since then not a single opera composer has, to put it mildly, equalled Wagner's lack of inhibition in language-creation. But many have shared his need to express something. This forces them to find a writer who is sufficiently in sympathy with what they want to say to be able to express it in his own words. That alone is not easy. If it comes off, the composer then has to hope that his writer will put the drama into a form that suits him. And this is not easy either, for even if the librettist has the best intentions and wants to produce something suited to opera, he has no idea of how to do it, for now that Wagner has broken the traditional mould, there is no longer any traditional opera-form. Finally, in an attempt to produce the desired literary merit, the modern librettist will probably clothe his opus in a sort of poetic diction which may hamper the composer by over-defining and anticipating the emotional interpretation of the text which should be the composer's job. Simple, not too colourful prose is more helpful to the composer and is also more likely to be understood by the audience. But the composer filled with an urge to express himself, may perhaps feel that he himself is capable of this kind of prose, thus justifying his decision to be his own librettist.

As against all this, it must be admitted that it is quite possible to enjoy an opera performance—up to a certain point, at least —without participating in the intellectual message, indeed without even grasping how the action fits together in practical terms. Obviously the intense musical interpretation of an emotion, presented through the singing and gestures of interestingly dressed mimes, is enough to interest spectators who have no idea what it all means. You can see and hear how an old man tortures himself to death with passionate self-laceration and slowly sinks on to a devout death-bed, and you can be deeply moved by this, even if you know nothing about the political problems of sixteenth-century Russia. This is probably why

Boris Godunov can be played so successfully in England and America—in any language but English.

Actually, the probabilities are that Anglo-Saxons' long-standing aversion to operas in English is not really due to the Italian singing teachers' prejudice that English is unsingable, but merely to those much deeper-rooted puritanical prejudices which until recently made Anglo-Saxons feel embarrassed when they understood the words of such a sinful and apparently peculiar entertainment as opera. If the greater emotional intensity that music creates was to be enjoyed or even borne, it was necessary to put a protective barrier of linguistic incomprehensibility in front of it.

Nevertheless it is still true that the best operas are those in which one can satisfactorily follow the text with one's logical and critical faculties *and* the emotional line with one's purely sensual powers of enjoyment. The obvious temptation is to let the logical content go altogether and portray only the emotion. This leads to the idea of 'abstract' opera, which has been attempted recently; in this the singers enjoy themselves, giving voice to appropriate but meaningless syllables so as to express certain emotions without their being motivated by a conventional 'plot'. But the venture does not seem very promising, because the audience will unhesitatingly consider it a hoax, if they are told what is going on. Only if they had no idea beforehand that they were to get nothing but 'tralala' or 'blohuhu' would such an experiment be worth making—only this could prove that the text 'does not matter'. As things are now, everyone is ready to ridicule the total confusion of the Trovatore-type libretto, but on the other hand everyone respects the total product and is even moved by it—simply because they know that at least one man took the whole farrago seriously—the composer. And that is what really matters.

23

WHAT ELECTRONIC MUSIC IS AND HOW IT IS MADE

IN my experience, most people, when they hear the words 'electronic music', think either of the breathy whine of the old-fashioned cinema organ or the sound effects which accompany the Mars rocket's landing on the forbidden planet in space films. The more advanced parties who already know of the twelve-tone technique and regard it as an intellectual perversion of nature, consider the efforts of electronic music to be the final, devilish degradation of the most spiritual of all arts, ground under the heel of mathematics and mechanics. As usual all the people who express these decided views have one quality in common: they do not know what they are talking about. This essay is an attempt to help them, so that they at least know what they are fighting.

Electronic music is made up of sounds that are not made by a man directly causing a substance to vibrate, but by electric impulses in vacuum tubes. Anybody who finds this 'mechanised' way of producing tone questionable, might bear in mind that the time-honoured organ is based on a similar (though not electric) principle. The organist does not blow his doubtless emotion-laden breath straight into the pipes, but presses down a key which operates a valve which lets a purely mechanically stored stream of air into the pipe. If the player wants to modify the timbre and volume of the tone so produced, he has to work other mechanical devices through which the size of the air-stream entering the pipe can be regulated or the stream can be introduced into a pre-arranged combination of pipes. Clearly, then, the organist only influences the sound indirectly via mechanical devices.

En passant it may be mentioned that electronic music differs from *musique concrète*, with which it has often been confused, in that it is fundamentally made up of electronically produced sounds. *Musique concrète*, as developed by a group in Paris, is essentially a montage of existing acoustic phenomena—bells, railway noises, fragments of human speech, animal noises and the like. These elements are recorded with a microphone, distorted by manipulating the tapes and put together in startling patterns. The effects are often provocative and sometimes interesting in the same way as the shock effects of Dada were interesting and, like Dada works, amusing for a short time. But these experiments have little in common with music as an art aiming at the organisation of tones.

Tone produced in a vacuum tube differs from all the tone produced by known musical instruments in having no overtones. If the layman says that in listening to a trumpet, say, he is not aware of any overtones but only the single note, he is right in so far as these overtones cannot be distinguished as individual sound-phenomena. Nevertheless they appear very clearly in the sense that it is they which give the trumpet its characteristic sound. If the same note were to be played with another group of overtones in the foreground everybody would say: 'That is a violin'. Given another 'spectrum' of overtones the connoisseur will immediately recognise his favourite tenor and the fact that he is singing 'ah'. (When he sings 'oo' the spectrum changes slightly.) Every way of producing sound known hitherto has had such a spectrum, because they were all based on causing some material to vibrate, and the different materials have different combinations of overtones. But electronically-produced tone has none. This can easily be demonstrated with the aid of an apparatus that makes the vibration-patterns of sound visible. While all conventional tones show complicated and irregular curves, electronic tone produces the symmetrical sine-curve familiar from geometry. Hence it is known as sinusoidal tone. Sinusoidal tone is the basic material of all music, and indeed of all acoustical phenomena in general —the atom of audible matter, so to speak. Everything we hear is made up of a mixture of sinus tones which combine in innumerable gradations of pitch and volume to form the billions of constellations of the audible cosmos. Only electronic tone-production has made it possible to isolate this atom from its complicated connections and allow us to hear it on its own. The far-reaching and revolutionary consequence of this is that we are now in a position to be able to make this atom enter into new combinations with other atoms—combinations not to be found in the existing world of sounds, which is dependent on the material make-up of vibrating bodies.

Our basic instrument is the frequency-generator, an iron box about the size of a small suitcase. With it we can produce sinusoidal tones of every number of vibrations within the limits of audibility and even outside them. Practically speaking, the lower limit of pure sinusoidal tone may be taken as 55 Hertz (i.e. 55 vibrations per second), which is three octaves below tuning A. Even lower notes can be heard, but only when overtones vibrate with them (as for example in the bottom octave on the piano). For musical purposes 5,000 H is a sufficiently high top limit. Many people can perceive notes up to 11,000 H, but in this stratosphere pitch can no longer be clearly distinguished— everything is just 'very high'.

The note an octave above our lowest note (55 H) has twice as many vibrations, 110. If we go up from this keynote in the conventional note-system, there are twelve different notes before we reach the A above. As we can register each vibration-number on the frequency-generator we have 55 different notes at our disposal between the lowest note and the one an octave above it. While we hear the notes as rising in a straight line, so that for example all octaves seem to cover acoustical areas of the same size, despite their absolute pitch, the vibration-numbers rise in a much steeper curve, so that the number of each note is twice as great as that of the one an octave below. Thus if our first octave goes from 55 to 110, the second goes from 110 to 220 and so on. Again, while previously we could only divide this second octave into twelve notes, we now have 110 different notes. Of course neither 110 nor even 55 notes in an octave can be distinguished so easily that they can be used in the kind of melody-structures we made with twelve notes. But it is easy to estimate what undreamed-of possibilities this opens up in the way of creating new sound-spectra by mixing so many separate notes.

By the way, these possibilities have long been known and the various instruments known under the collective name of 'electric organs'—the regrettably christened 'novachords' and 'orgatrons' and even 'claviolines'—are all based on this principle. But they got in the way of the development of real electronic music because their inventors were not interested in a new world of sounds but only in imitating the old one synthetically. The electronic instrument was only worth the money if its tone could not be distinguished from a real violin, trumpet or what have you, and it tried to justify itself by pointing out that you only needed to press a button to get seven different timbres, thus enabling the instrument's owner to economise on the wages of six musicians. This has nothing to do with electronic music.

To sum up the acoustical aspects: we know that we can produce thousands of musical atoms, or sinusoidal tones, within the limits of audibility. What are we doing with these tones? One cannot play on a frequency-generator as on a piano because it only produces one note at a time; nor is it like a flute, because after each note the dials have to be re-set to produce the next frequency. In order to make music out of this basic material, the notes must first be captured in some way.

This is where we call on second technical innovation essential for true electronic music: tape-recording. That vacuum tubes produce notes has long been known, as aforesaid. But before a method of recording these sounds had been found, the tubes had to be built into an apparatus like an organ with a keyboard if it was to be played. The limitations of this arrangement are obvious: exactly as with the traditional organ one has to be content with a certain number of predetermined combinations, and there are severe technical restrictions on the changes from one combination to another that one can make during performance.

But now the notes and sounds we produce are recorded straight on to tape. There is no microphone, as when a violinist, say, records something; the electric impulses of the frequency-generator go directly to the input of the tape-recorder. The tape, then, is the place where the music we want to make is gradually stored as we get it from our sound-sources. But the tape is also the means by which our music becomes audible. The music is 'performed' by playing the tape. So the tape represents both the composition and the performance. That is, composition and performance are identical. What we record on the tape is the music. It does not need later 'performance' by musicians—in fact, it cannot have it, for it does not exist off the tape. And this tape is really a magic device. Even after ample experience it is impossible to estimate just what one can do with this modest half-inch-wide strip of dull-looking brown material to produce sound effects that could not be achieved in any other way.

First, the sound composed of the frequency-generator's sinusoidal tones can be manipulated in many ways. For example, the volume of each note of a sound can be gradated most delicately and precisely, and a series of changing sound-patterns can be produced by this alone. With devices that work like filters, and so, reasonably enough, are called filters, certain frequency-areas can be brought out while others disappear into the background, so that the sound gains luminosity or sinks into darkness. If the tape on which the sound is recorded is cut obliquely, smooth insertions can be made, whereas rectangular cuts give hard, percussive attacks. If a sound that begins like this is quickly faded out (that is, the input-unit is quickly switched off) one gets a percussive note; if more slowly faded out, the note dies away more gently. A really three-dimensional echo can be obtained by using the echo-chamber, an ordinary empty room in which the sound is emitted by a loudspeaker and recaptured together with the room's reverberations, by a microphone opposite. This 'signal' returns immediately (at the speed of light) to the studio and we can put in more or less echo. We can start the sound 'dry' and then gradually add more and more echo. We can filter the echo so that, say, the lower notes gradually fall out of the echoing sound and finally only the high ones sound as an echo. We can cut the 'dry' beginning of the sound out of the tape, or wipe it off, so that only the echo (of nothing, so to speak) remains floating in space. And we can run the tape backwards so that we get an increasing echo, starting from nothing, which suddenly breaks off. By arranging the feedback in a certain way we can make the sound shake at regular intervals. We can play this result three octaves higher on a machine for the purpose. At this pitch the sound becomes thin and cutting and the slow shaking goes eight times as fast, producing an effect of aggressive vehemence. Many, many more things could be added to the list of what one can do with a simple sinusoidal note by manipulating the recording machine. It may be of interest that very costly equipment is by no means necessary. All the phenomena I have described come only from an extremely intelligent, inventive use of standard machinery which, as far as I know has only been elaborated in the electronic studio of the West German Radio in Cologne.

The layman has already heard many of these effects behind the aforementioned space-ship in the cinema or on television. They are improvised by technicians experimenting with the brown tape in the still watches of the night. It needs the composer to discover how this enormous mass of sound material can be turned to account in presenting musical ideas. In this lies the real importance of the great precision with which musical time-relationships can be regulated by means of tape. It must be remembered that modern music, particularly the music developed on the basis of atonal expressionism, is very complicated rhythmically. In other words, the segments of time between the single events of a musical passage are irregular in length and often distinguished only by very minute differences. Although it is crucially important to the musical idea for these time-relationships to be absolutely accurate, they give performers, particularly ensembles, a great deal of difficulty. The rehearsal work necessary is often out of all proportion to the result, which in the final analysis depends on the unforeseeable nervous condition of the performers at the moment of performance, and so is threatened by considerable uncertainty factors.

Producing the music on tape disposes of all these difficulties at one blow. The duration of a note or any other musical unit is expressed by the length of the bit of tape on which it is recorded. This length depends in its turn on the speed at which the tape goes through the recording apparatus. So far the best results in electronic recordings have been obtained with the maximum speed on normal machines—76 cm. per second: a note that lasts one second takes up 76 cm. of tape. Of course the tape can be cut accurately to a millimetre. But even if we content ourselves with distances of one centimetre, time-differences of one-seventysixth of a second can be accurately presented. This is a much smaller difference than the human ear can perceive. It has been proved experimentally that when, for example, a sequence of four notes whizzes past above a certain speed limit the ear can no longer distinguish the order in which the notes come. Normally time-differences of, say, one-twentieth of a second are enough to produce considerable effect, musically speaking. It would be arrogant, cruel, and, in any case, hopeless to suggest to a group of musicians that one should begin at the beginning of a second, the second three-twentieths, the third twelve-twentieths and the fourth seventeen-twentieths later, while the first perhaps plays another note ten-twentieths after his first.

With the aid of tape the problem can be solved without fear and trembling. The second note must go past the recording head 12 cm. after the first, the third 48 cm., and the fourth 68 cm. after, while the first player's second note is recorded 40 cm. after zero. It is child's play to measure off these distances, cut the tape into the correct lengths and stick the pieces together in the right order.

The problem becomes more difficult with musical processes progressing simultaneously. After all, music does not consist merely of a sequence of single notes. With simultaneous processes the musical progress must be split into horizontal layers which must be organised so that the maximum number of successive elements in the complex are got into each layer without 'overlapping'. For one layer, but only one, can be recorded on a single tape without difficulty. The next layer goes on another tape, and so on. After all the layers have been recorded they have to be synchronised: each tape is so placed in its own machine that when all the machines begin to play simultaneously the tapes all play at the moment required for the composition. All the machines are connected to a recording machine which records the total result on a new tape. If this *sounds* complicated it is much more so in reality. The ingenuity and inventiveness of the technicians who carry out these synchronisation-processes cannot be too much admired. Without reliable and, to a certain extent, manageable synchronisation-systems, electronic music would have to remain no more than a dream.

As I have said, the precision of this machinery is attractive above all because it makes it possible to 'perform' limitless irregularities. So the total determinacy of machines serves to create a symbol of complete freedom. This is not to be confused with the 'agogic nuances' which make a human performer's playing appear to be 'living'. (The new science of communications, cybernetics, to whose thought-processes electronic musicians rightly feel attracted, calls these irregularities 'aleatoric elements'—from the Latin *alea*, dice, because they are really only statistically determinable chance-results.) When, in an 'inspired' performance of sixteen bars of Beethoven, no two bars are exactly the same length, although the composer has not indicated any differences, the hearer is not conscious of the differences: if he was, the performance would not be 'inspired' but distorted. The listener is principally conscious of the dominant regularity of the structure and feels it to be 'living' because of the imperceptible variations. The structures of new music are irregular *a priori*, so that the intrusion of aleatoric elements, above a certain point, can easily make them unrecognisable.

Total mastery of great complexity is a perfectly legitimate art-ideal. It principally attracts those composers who are concerned to 'generalise' the serial principle derived from the later twelve-tone technique. Not only the sequence of intervals between the notes of the basic pattern but the time-sequence of the events (the rhythm), their relative volume and every aspect of the musical organism is governed by a pre-selected system of measurements and proportions. This system is called a 'row' in the broadest sense of the word. (There is more medievalism in this concept than many of its supporters would admit.) If the measurements selected are not trivial—if they are, the whole exercise is not worth the trouble—there emerge results so complex that only electronic performance can guarantee that they will be faultlessly carried out. With the strange and wonderful dialectic that runs through this, as through all human endeavours, this knife-edge accuracy often sounds like the triumph of the aleatorical. This is, of course, due to its complexity. The same dialectic makes the machine, apparently a totally rationalised medium, the ideal field for real compositorial improvisation. A musician who improvises at the piano is not composing, but using certain fabric-making procedures which have emerged from experience in order to pursue a musical idea for a while in a playful, non-obligatory way. (Beethoven who, it is recorded, was an exciting improviser, worked for years on a phrase when he was composing.)

Now the electronic musician can work as directly on his material as the painter or sculptor. You cannot say to the brass in a rehearsal: 'Please try to play that a little later—say about half a second'. But it is very easy to shift a tape in the synchronisation so that the note arrives 32 or 38 or 42 cm. later. The aleatoric element is no longer the function of an individual 're-creating' the music, but the direct expression of its creator's imagination. At some point on the far horizon the lines of freely chosen assumption and assumptionless free choice meet.

A tangled prospect? We are still at the very beginning of it all.

24

ON THE AGEING AND OBSOLESCENCE
OF MUSIC

IT is really only the avant-garde snobs, for whom nothing can
be esoteric enough, and the professional producers of light
music who smile pityingly at the mere idea of 'opus music',
who believe that music becomes obsolete. I have heard publishers discussing the commercial potential of a popular song
in Hollywood and their main objection was: 'Nice idea, but
there is not a single 1956 chord in it.' But I also remember
hearing certain Parisian pioneers of the most abstract modernity
dismissing a new work with the remark that 'The man just has
no idea that we are writing in 1925. One might have been able
to swallow this in 1920 . . .'

Although the two products were entirely different, much the
same ideas lay behind both criticisms. The realisation that we
live in a world of constant change has grown to a kind of
impotent frenzy, and this frenzy has produced in both the pace-
makers of modernity and the style-setters of fashion a terrible
fear that, if they do not ruthlessly denounce the arteriosclerosis
of yesterday, they may be left behind in the march of progress.
Our civilisation is kinetic in character—Oswald Spengler called
its urge towards continual change 'Faustian'—and in the above
outlook the realisation of this fact curiously goes hand in hand
with the idea that each phase has a rigidly defined form of expression which becomes meaningless as soon as we enter the
next phase. This attitude is so geared to the superficial attractions deriving from the equipment of music that it overlooks
the ageing which affects the actual substance of music, its artistic
processes and stylistic principles.

The pop-music producers, burning the midnight oil, not to speak of innumerable cigars and whisky-calories, to find their 1956 chords on the piano, would be surprised and disappointed to learn that their brand-new, up-to-the-minute models were well known in 1856. Luckily musical history begins for them with Gershwin and so there is still a great deal left for them to discover. It is perhaps more serious that the 1956 vintage varies hardly at all from those of '55, '54, and '53. But in reality this is quite all right as the public basically always wants the same thing. It is only persuaded to think it wants something new so that pop-production can keep going. Every hit is extolled as something 'different'. But if it is a success, this is principally due to the fact that it is not at all different but exactly the same. What really pleases the average listener is not discovering something new, but recognising something he has known for a long time. And the real art of pop-composition lies in arranging a work in such a way that the very first encounter with it stimulates recognition. Once you realise how difficult this is, you cannot help respecting the composers who indefatigably attempt it over and over again.

We know only too well that the majority of 'serious' listeners, too, prefer the happy experience of recognition to the adventure of discovery. This is bitterly complained of by composers whose music is an adventure: for unlike their colleagues in the popular branch they are trying to write music that really is 'different' from its predecessors. To the public at large favourite pieces never grow stale, or only so slowly that the process does not keep pace with the 'progress' claimed by composers. But even though the average listener remains devoted to a group of styles of the past, huge quantities of music become so obsolescent that they disappear out of the consciousness of the present day almost completely. This is probably because in the course of time, the most mature and original forms of a past

222

style become rooted in the public mind and squeeze out the inferior examples. When you have Schumann and Mendelssohn as examples of German Romanticism, composers such as Marschner and Spohr look 'outmoded'—perhaps unjustly. Richard Strauss and, say, Pfitzner, represent a certain trend so strikingly that beside them people like Thuille and Nicodé appear obsolete. It would be easy to add more examples.

It is only in the last hundred years or so that this nostalgic attachment to a few styles of the past has become typical. Only for about a century has there existed the so-called 'classical repertoire', that complete and closed stock of cultural goodies which are presented again and again to delight the ear and stop people from really getting to know contemporary work. Before then it was quite the other way round: it was taken for granted that every occasion for hearing music would chiefly provide new music; works from the past were only played occasionally—on the whole, they were the exceptions.

No doubt it would be ridiculous to assume that the public has changed altogether and that a collection of eager-to-learn progressives has turned into a mob of lazy reactionaries. True, the public has changed, particularly by becoming much larger. If, as often happens in America, a 5,000- or 6,000-seat hall has to be sold out just to cover the costs of a concert, obviously the programme has to reckon with a different common denominator of curiosity and perceptiveness than if an attraction for 300-400 experts is being prepared. But even connoisseurs enjoy feeling the Aha! of recognition; indeed their expertise consists mainly of being able to single out the fine nuances of even minute divergences from the norm lurking in a forest of well-known characteristics. In this regard the 'new' music of past ages made it easier for them than the music of today, for the new elements then did not appear in such a drastic way, revolutionising the material and the procedure at the same time, as has happened with ever-increasing rapidity and intensity in the last decades. It is understandable that in the eighteenth century, when the vocabulary, style and forms of music were not exposed to any sudden and radical upheavals, people enjoyed a large number of individually differentiated variations of a more or less constant range of ideas and so kept on demanding new variations of this kind. This well explains why in those happier days much more contemporary music was absorbed than today, and why at that time there was no question of the damming-up of past art-sources which is now called the 'repertoire'.

In the meanwhile music has undergone such basic changes that the well-known features of the old can only be recognised with difficulty in the new, if they can be recognised at all. At the same time the really well informed connoisseurs among the public have shrunk to a vanishing minority, while the dominant majority consists of passive 'pleasure-seekers'. But even they develop the capacity to appreciate fine nuances within the field of static experience. Nowadays, however, this capacity is no longer directed towards the music itself, which has long passed the borders of foreseeability and so made recognition impossible; it is applied almost entirely to nuances of performance. The composer, who from the very nature of his subject is a specialist in musical substance, often feels bored or useless (according to mood and situation) when he notices how laymen who have not the smallest idea of the simplest facts of compositional construction, can discuss the relative merits of a Beethoven performance by, say, Furtwängler, Koussevitsky or Toscanini with accuracy, authority and eloquence. The pleasure in being able to appreciate such nuances probably corresponds to that felt by eighteenth-century listeners when they compared how Haydn, Dittersdorf, Mozart, Clementi, J. C. Bach and numerous others dealt with the problem of sonata form. The present pre-occupation with the finesses of performance also explains why the record industry finds it profitable to market a handful of classical masterpieces in fifty or more different versions, while the sporadic recordings of new music drag out an unenviable existence as white elephants.

The more stubbornly the wide public clings to traditional values, the more passionately modernists pursue progress, impatiently throwing on the junk heap the inventions that only a little while ago were considered bold pointers to the future. At first sight one might think that the composers who are intent on developing new ways of composing and complain that the public will have nothing to do with their products would hail such assistance with satisfaction. But this is not so. The tendency to disavow yesterday's advances, call them 'old-fashioned', has not the slightest influence on the mind of a public that composedly enjoys the work of the day before yesterday. As the official apparatus of music-distribution is almost entirely geared to this public, most performances of new music take place in an atmosphere dominated by specialists—composers, critics, musicologists, students, musical executive organs, conductors and the like. In the main, however, these specialists do not go to an art-work for a total emotional experience; they are interested in the demonstration of new materials, new principles of composition, procedures, methods. The broader application of such achievements to a large number of subjects worth writing and presenting interests them less than the unique experimental demonstration of the invention. This creates the danger of a radicalisation that will accelerate continuously, ending in a sad cul-de-sac where perhaps even the unique experiment will hardly be worthwhile because it can already be considered out of date before it has even happened.

Now a work of art does not consist only of equipment and procedure; these are common to many others of its own kind and links it to the stylistic pattern of the age. It draws its validity from the uniqueness of the vision which these basic elements serve; this is what makes it stand out above its age, according to the force and vitality of the vision. If a critic, reviewing a performance of Schoenberg's *Gurrelieder*, says that such 'sickly music' can no longer be accepted, this harsh judgment means something in so far as much (though not all) of Schoenberg's early work may seem 'sickly' to a taste that feels at home with the astringent, jagged sounds and fissured structures of later music. But to call such a work 'obsolete' for that reason, is throwing out the baby with the bathwater. At the high tide of Wagnerianism there were those who called Mozart 'obsolete' because the outward form of his music seemed like a thin, childish tinkle beside the colossal quantities Wagner set in motion. As we have seen, Wagner did not have the last word and Mozart no longer strikes us as 'outmoded'.

In all reason, then, we must accept that what in many circles is specifically (and absolutely) called New Music—i.e. the styles developed at the beginning of the century by Schoenberg and under his influence, reaching their peak between the two wars —will not have the last word either. Although the vital works will never become obsolete, whatever style they are written in, the philosophical and technical constructions that play a crucial role in the composition of these works are subject to the same ageing process that nothing escapes in a 'Faustian', dynamic culture.

However, the fact that 'New Music', too, grows old does not mean that it must become senile, but, probably, that the im- pulses in it lead to new formulas of a different sort. T. W. Adorno, one of the most acute and articulate spokesmen of 'New Music' seems to incline to the first, pessimistic interpre- tation, as he sees only error and decline in what more optimistic observers see as a new formulation. In his essay 'Music and

Language' and in an earlier lecture 'The Ageing of New Music' Adorno has made up his mind that music is like language. He underpins this thesis with convincing arguments and then says: 'The movement summed up under the name of New Music might easily be presented as a collective allergy to the primacy of language-similarity. Of course it is just its most radical manifestations that follow an extreme of language-similarity rather than that anti-language impulse.' This shows up the dialectical tension between the expressionistic release of vehement expressive energies and the way the twelve-tone technique sharply disciplines the compositional process—two tendencies that apparently work against each other and which are constantly interacting in later 'New Music'. The latest experiments in composition, following the age of New Music, seem to restore the balance between the two tendencies in so far as they give overriding importance to the 'regular' aspect by extending and generalising the serial principle of the twelve-tone technique in a 'totalitarian' way. It is above all the opening up of the electronic medium that has made this a possible and obvious development. Adorno sees this as an 'attempt to remove music's language-similarity' and eliminate the 'subject'—that is, the free creative spirit—from music; its place is filled by 'integral rationalisation': 'This is not to deny that a suggestive power derives from the structures it produces—the suggestive power which is characteristic of everything consistent, even if it is absurd. But we are moving towards the absurd. These pieces are, in the strict sense, musically meaningless . . . . What is the point of such a very purified type of music? When the dominant principle is that elements are handled as atoms the concept of musical coherence falls to pieces, and without it there can really be no question of music.'

The 'integral rationalisation' that may well be considered the final aim of these recent efforts has still not been achieved. As far as I can judge, the existing works in the extended serial technique—whether electronic or for conventional sound-producers—contain many more aleatoric elements than might appear, from the theory, which is a good deal ahead of its practical application. (Aleatoric, in the 'rationalists'' usage, means dependent on chance or, in the usage of the advocates of New Music, set free from the 'subject'.) But even if the 'integral rationalisation' succeeds and everything is 'calculated' in advance down to the last detail, there must be a 'subject' to do the calculations. Even the most formidable electronic computer can only calculate what a man gives it to calculate.

We who have grown up with the 'language-similarity' of music may have difficulty in imagining the point of a music 'purged' of all such similarity. But the fact that we find it difficult to answer this question does not mean that there is no answer. It is conceivable that the relationship between music and language that seems so evident and natural to us can really be put into or taken out of many musical forms but is not necessarily a *sine qua non* for all these forms. It *is* a *sine qua non* of the music we are familiar with since about the Renaissance. But much in medieval music and the music of other non-Occidental cultures may be founded on quite different basic assumptions. And one can conceive it possible that what we call 'musical coherence' is a mode of apperception particularly suited to our mental structure, and that alongside it there may be other characteristics which would make musical utterances seem meaningful to minds constructed differently.

It is not only New Music but we who made it who grow old. But as yet we are not so old that we cannot remember how those who wanted to prove the existing situation absolute, adducing 'unshakeable' arguments, told us that our efforts were absurd. And we had excellent arguments with which we proved the reverse. The 'row' on which this world's life is organised by the divine computer at least allows us, as 'free subjects' to select our old-age symptoms. We can become more dogmatic or less dogmatic. I prefer the 'lesser' evil and choose as my symptom the conviction that things will go on even if at first they strike me as absurd.

CONVERSATION PAST MIDNIGHT

'In Ciro's, a plushy night-spot in Mexico City, the band beat out a rumba rhythm . . . *La Bamba*. The young American who leads the band at Ciro's . . . orchestrated the simple folk melody . . . Socialites, free-spending European expatriates and American travellers were calling for nothing but *La Bamba*. . .'

'No Negro has ever sung or been invited to sing a principal rôle in the Metropolitan Opera. . . Jovial Kentucky-born Robert Todd Duncan, 41, has never given up hope of getting into grand opera . . . taught singing . . . floundered through a jive film . . . made his début . . . praise of his singing . . .'

A column and a half about *La Bamba* and a column on the rise of Robert Todd Duncan (under the title 'Porgy to Pagliacci'), that comprises the music section of *Time Magazine* of October 8, 1945. The musician, who, during this week learned some very sad news (not through the newspapers, incidentally, but by word of mouth) is surprised to find no trace of it in the magazine that takes pride in gathering, editing, interpreting and publishing all the important events of the week. But he finds it after all a few pages further on in the column called 'Milestones', which summarises all the facts of life (and death) considered worthy of inclusion in a weekly survey:

'Died: Béla Bartók, 64, prolific Hungarian composer of piquant, sometimes cacophonous orchestral and chamber music; long-time student of Magyar and Jugoslav folk music; after long illness; in Manhattan, his home since 1940. A radical modernist, Bartók in 1938 wrote Rhapsody for Clarinet and Violin especially for his friend Joseph Szigéti's violin and Benny Goodman's rippling clarinet.'

For the musician these seven lines are almost as shattering as the news they report. It seems to him that the catastrophe which dried up for ever one mighty stream of living music should have been included among the musical news rather than in the personal column. In his agitation he gives way to the temptation to subject the dialectic of the term 'news' to a critical analysis. Obviously the mere death of a composer is not musical news, since it does not represent a musical event such as the launching of a new dance at Ciro's in Mexico City or the assumption of a particular rôle by a Negro singer. It might have been different if the composer had died after dedicating a new work to Frank Sinatra or at least while bringing out a new piece of cacophony. If we understand it rightly, the final and irrevocable loss of his power to bring out any more new pieces is not news only for the reason that in the act of dying he did not use that power. Since, however, he had used it on occasions in the past, his death is noted, albeit in a different context. There is reason to believe that Bartók owed this passing mention only to the fact that one of his works could be coupled with Benny Goodman's 'rippling clarinet'. For though the Hungarian master is dubbed prolific, no other individual work of his is named, and the one thus singled out is accorded three of the whole seven lines of the obituary.

Philosophic analysis of the theoretical principles of journalism is perhaps no occupation for a troubled mind, and the result of our examination may not amount to very much. All the same it does seem that to be news, something unfamiliar (and in particular unexpected) must make contact with something very familiar and usual. By this standard the assassination of any well-known public figure always has an unsurpassable news value. In the present case the news value is obviously small; at the time of his death Béla Bartók was not widely known, at least not among the readers of *Time Magazine*; the sad event was not connected with any unusual circumstances, such as a fall from a flying aeroplane, for instance, in which case the minus point of the relative obscurity of the victim would have been counterbalanced by the plus of the 'unfamiliar' factor, that is to say, the sensational nature of the accident. (Not Béla Bartók himself but Death would in this case have been the 'familiar' element making effective contact with the unfamiliar.) Since it did not happen like that, the victim's very lack of popularity must have appeared of more moment and to have raised the importance of the popularity factor on the other side of the scale. This was obviously the thought process of the man who wrote those seven lines. The terms 'piquant, sometimes cacophonous', 'radical modernist', as well as the reference to the music of remote countries wrap the man concerned in an interesting veil of obscurity (not interesting enough, however, to give him or even his death 'news value'). And then, as a contrast to all that, he is suddenly brought into contact with something very familiar—with Benny Goodman's 'rippling clarinet'. News is therefore, it appears, something that is basically not new at all.

My journalist friend, who has for some time been looking over my shoulder with growing impatience, can contain himself no longer. 'Who cares about your definition of news and your reasons for making it? As far as I am concerned news is what interests the two million readers of my magazine.'

'And how do you know what interests them?'

'Above all by knowing what interests me. As a person of average intelligence, good general education, normal taste and commonsense, I can be held typical of the majority of my readers. And on top of that we have polls, statistics, circulars, letters from subscribers . .'

'Has it never occurred to you that the way in which people react might depend very largely on what you and others like you put into their minds? As you ask, so shall you be answered.'

'Maybe. But what are you grumbling about? What should we have written about your friend Bartók in place of that notice you so much disapprove of?'

'You might have mentioned the fact that he is an immortal composer.'

'A what? Are you telling me that he never really died? Has someone been trying out a new drug on him to bring him back to life? You know that story about Aldous Huxley, don't you —the one with the swan? That really was news.'

'No, no. You know perfectly well what I mean.'

'Yes, you mean all that symbolic stuff. His music will outlast his own time and so on. Well, maybe it will. But that isn't news, it's not fact. It's publishers' puff material.'

'No, it isn't, my friend. It's my own sincere opinion.'

'Forgive me for saying it, but your opinion isn't news either.'

'Then how would it be if you yourself had an opinion for a change—and expressed it?'

'Sorry, old man, but that's not what I'm paid for. My job is to find out what interests two million people, or at any rate as many of them as possible. And if that's La Bamba—well, La Bamba it is. But if you really want my own opinion, you can have it. I say that if two million people are interested in knowing something about La Bamba, then it certainly must be interesting.'

'But you must see that, if it *does* interest them, that can only be because you have given them something to read about it. Before that they didn't even know of the existence of La Bamba. The fact that they know it now is your doing, and you are stunned by a quantity which you yourself have brought about quite artificially. From an objective point of view your Bamba rates not more but infinitely less in terms of interest than my Béla Bartók.'

'What exactly do you understand by objective point of view? There's nothing more objective than the fact that millions of people listen to Benny Goodman playing *La Bamba* on his rippling clarinet. Only very few listen to the music of Béla Bartók.'

'Because it's so rarely played.'

'Then hadn't you better talk to your friends the conductors, the violinists and the pianists? If they can make news with Bartók I shall gladly report it. Good night.'

So I had a talk with my friend the conductor. 'Let us keep right off personal things,' he implored me, 'and talk about contemporary music as a whole. Personally I was a great admirer of Bartók, and I should feel less inhibited if I didn't have to relate myself to him.'

'Just as you like. But could your inhibitions be due in any way to the feeling that you would hesitate to grant Bartók the tribute of immortality?'

'I would hesitate to grant that to any contemporary composer. Only time can decide whether a composer has achieved immortality. We can call him immortal if his work manages to stand up against the competition resulting from a constant succession of other works.'

'And how does a work stand up against such competition?'

'By holding its place in the repertoire of public concerts, that is to say, when people keep on demanding to hear it in spite of the flood of new material which is constantly being put forward.'

'That answer raises a whole number of questions which seem to me to need clarifying. In the first place, how do people make their demands known? And secondly, is the number of performances the only measure of immortality—is it indeed even an acceptable one?'

'Those are not quite the questions I expected. People make their demands for particular works known by buying larger numbers of tickets when they are played than they buy when other works are advertised. At least I suppose that is what happens. My manager keeps figures on it, he gets letters from people and so on.'

'But how do the people who write the letters and buy the tickets know exactly what they are after? Are they so thoroughly conversant with what is available that they are in a position to choose properly?'

'No, of course not. They are only expressing their preference for some of the works that have been put in front of them.'

'So if—at the request of your manager, I suppose—you perform only those compositions for which a preference has been expressed, your audiences never get a chance to form anything like an enlightened judgment. The result is that some pieces get played over and over again. You consider these pieces immortal because your audiences favour them, and the audiences favour them in the belief that you play them because they are immortal. How's that for a vicious circle?'

'Well, it's a disturbing thought, but happily you exaggerate. In fact my concerts include quite a number of contemporary works which are on nobody's list. My manager doesn't like it particularly, I admit, but I do it all the same, though of course I have to use a lot of discretion.'

'And as a result of your discretion, people are warned from the very start not to expect anything like the star pieces of your repertoire, the recognised immortal masterpieces. Vacillating sponsorship of this sort means that new works scarcely stand a chance of figuring again in another programme, and that adds to the impression that they are not of lasting value. As you see, we composers have grounds enough to bother ourselves about immortality.'

'Is it quite fair to call our support of new music vacillating? More than one conductor has risked his position by championing new music.'

'But hardly one of them has ever lost it.'

'And if he had lost it, what good would that have done you?'

'Well, maybe there isn't much point in discussing the uses of a martyr. But the more deeply you get involved in the conflict between your own convictions and the views of your management, the more you acknowledge that there are other standards of measurement beyond the number of performances and the number of listeners.'

'Of course the value of a piece doesn't depend on how often I can put it in my programmes. There are many works which I should like to play more often than others which I am obliged to play. But possibly these very worthwhile works would not get themselves established even then: perhaps they are just not tough enough to overcome all the obstacles which time and circumstances put in the way of anything new.'

'In other words immortality is a kind of survival of the fittest, which is not necessarily always the most valuable. A depressing thought, particularly since what you call time and circumstances could be controlled simply enough by people in your position who have the ability to recognise worth when they see it and give it its proper due.'

'I should say that immortality is too big a word for the sort of thing we are talking about here. Are you not simply stating that some works keep their place in the repertoire for a time following their first performance? As far as I can see, about two hundred years appears to be the maximum life of any composition.'

'You are basing that, I suppose, on the fact that no music

earlier than Bach's ever appears in your programmes. So I take it you consider the music of early composers, let us say Palestrina, Lasso, Josquin des Près, is not immortal?'

'In a certain sense of the word it's immortal of course. But clearly it doesn't "live" in the same way as Schubert or Chopin. Maybe we ought to acknowledge two different kinds of immortality: one based on the support of the mob and the other confined to the recognition of a minority of experts, connoisseurs and amateurs.'

'Well, that's true as far as it goes. But there must surely be a wider conception, one in which all these various possibilities can be accommodated. The case of Béla Bartók upset me so, you understand, because I am convinced that he is a part of immortality, whatever that may be, and in his own time that has gone largely unrecognised. If immortality, however far we push the idea into symbolic regions, means anything at all, then surely it must have something to do with eternity. What is exercising me is the question of how this participation in eternity can be recognised in the earthly existence of the immortals.'

'I am afraid that that question is entirely outside the very earthly province in which I live and have my being. Perhaps you should have a word with your friend the philosopher.'

And so I consulted my friend the philosopher. 'The problem that taxes me,' I said, 'is concerned with the conception of values. The term "lasting value" is nowadays sorely abused. Every new book appearing on the market is labelled by its publisher as a work of lasting value. Going to the other extreme, a music critic whose pathological reaction to new music is nothing but blind and meaningless hatred can imagine that he is dealing a new work a mortal blow if he asserts that it will not last. His words are not, of course, endowed with the power of magic, and the cases in which history has proved such prophecies wrong are so numerous and so notorious that one

238

finds it hard to conceive how any critic in his right senses can still make such predictions. But no doubt you realise that verdicts of this kind, however impertinent, can hurt a composer more deeply than any genuine discussion of aesthetic or technical failings, for the reason that nothing worries him so much as concern about the fate of his work in a more distant future. Most composers are eager to see their works performed as often as possible, The reason is clear enough, and many are content to look no further: they are overjoyed to hear their works and they know that performances bring financial rewards in the shape of royalties. But I am certain that there is another motive as compelling, if not even more compelling than these. A composer feels he has the chance of being recognised by posterity only if he has not been disregarded in his own time. He feels that the illustrious spirits of the past, whose ubiquity seems to block his way wherever he turns, have the advantage over him on account of the fact that their music was often played while they were themselves still in the land of the living, and is still played so frequently because it affected its own time. We know, of course, that even in the time of the great masters huge wads of rubbish were foisted on the public and that a lot of it was very much more successful and famous than the works we admire today. All the same, it seems that the appreciation of true value was more widespread then than it is today. It is almost inconceivable that a highly regarded weekly could in 1827 have published a notice like this:

'Died: Ludwig van Beethoven, deaf, quarrelsome, slovenly composer of symphonies and quartets, of which many think highly; after long illness; in Vienna. Beethoven won general acclaim with a piece depicting the victory of Wellington over the one-time dictator Napoleon Bonaparte, which was inspired by Beethoven's friend Mälzel, distinguished, ingenious inventor of a ticking time-beating machine.'

'Stop', cried the philosopher with a laugh. 'I don't yet see what all this has to do with philosophy. Perhaps it could be put down simply to changes in the social structure or to other historical factors. But these don't really go to the root of your problem, nor do they have very much to do with music, which was the subject we wanted to talk about.'

'What are you trying to say? That value has nothing to do with value-forming experience? That there are colours which nobody can see?'

'Perhaps we needn't go into such subtleties in order to reach agreement between ourselves that the sort of value you are speaking of existed at times and in places in which nobody identified himself with your particular standards. I remember you once spoke to me about certain composers whose work was almost completely forgotten for a long time and then rediscovered when a new appreciation of their greatness emerged. Maybe you can jog my memory with a few names.'

'The most famous instance is Johann Sebastian Bach. His music, considered today to be one of the peaks of Western culture, was hardly played at all for nearly a century after his death. And some of Schubert's best-known pieces were not performed at all during his lifetime and were discovered only many years later. Various composers of earlier days had a similar, if less dramatic, fate.'

'Exactly. All this suggests that the immortality of these composers does not depend on the number of people who at some time or other came into contact with their music, nor on any other quantity factor of that kind. It must rather be the special quality of their works that distinguishes them from other compositions. The fact that these works have remained alive for centuries and have constantly reasserted their power over each succeeding generation percipient enough to grasp their message —this is maybe incidental to their special distinction.'

'And how would you define this special distinction?'

'I suppose I should be flattered that you address this question to me. It is really more your business to bring up technical arguments to show a layman like myself in what way your Bach, your Schubert, your Palestrina are more excellent than others and so win the badge of immortality.'

'I could do that, certainly. But I feel that immortality and excellence are not really related ideas, though they may coincide in practice.'

'There you are right. When you were speaking of the origins of the composer's desire to have his works performed I was reminded of a lecture by Jacques Maritain in which he said something like this—it was a long time ago and I quote from memory: "Fundamentally the artist does not want to convince but to endure".'

'Ah, yes, that's quite a thought. For those of us who encounter such huge obstacles in our attempts to convince mankind it's quite a comfort. But the snag is that the artist can endure only when he has succeeded in convincing his contemporaries.'

'Well, he will always convince some of them. But that is by the way. It's not they whom he wants to convince: the genius wants to convince God, and that is his way of enduring.'

'What do you mean by that?'

'In his great moments the genius brings forth something that reflects eternal truth, the sort of truth to which we cannot attain by ourselves, which comes only to saints in moments of revelation. An artist's work belongs of course wholly in this world, but all the same it can catch a glimpse of the other world, of the eternal. And in doing so it partakes of immortality.'

'Would a work of this sort have to be on a religious subject?'

'No, not at all. But it would have to spring from a religious impulse on the part of its creator. Can you recall what Kierkegaard said about genius? "In general a genius differs from other men only in that in his historical circumstances he perceives his origin as directly as Adam. Every time a genius is born it is as if existence as such is laid in the balance, for he reviews and experiences the whole of the past until he reaches himself." It is this staking all, this starting again from the beginning and yet being filled with the whole richness of historical experience that distinguishes the work of a genius.'

'Is there any recognisable mark of this distinction in the work itself, or must we accept the word of its creator as assurance of the proper state of mind? Or do we draw our own conclusions from the impression that the work makes on us?'

'Obviously the author's claim is not enough of itself, otherwise every dilettante will assure us that in the creation of his work he has been dwelling in the highest regions, and that might be so from a subjective point of view. Our own reaction to the work might be somewhat more convincing, but we must not forget that the most extraordinary productions of genius were not recognised as such when they were new. Perhaps it is this very extraordinariness which is the surest criterion of immortality.'

'You are no doubt aware of the usual objection that not everything that is different is necessarily excellent.'

'That may be true if it is at the same time not significant as well.'

'But it is exactly the significance which people don't recognise when something is different, because it does not satisfy conventional ideas of significance.'

'Therein lies the risk that the creator of extraordinary things must take on himself. He is in a similar position to the man who feels the call to become a saint. As you know, practically every saint has stood in danger of being condemned as a heretic. Superficially that might be put down to the short-sighted conservatism of the church, but I believe that in order to become a saint a man must go through a crisis that brings him in any case to the borderline of heresy. In certain of its aspects the work of a genius is very closely akin to the miracle which a saint performs. A miracle is also a part of this world and its direct result is transitory. The deaf man who is given back his hearing must one day die, and the fact of the miracle has then vanished. Certainly the miracle could never have been performed without the aid of supernatural powers, and after it the world is no longer the same, even when the cause of its change is forgotten. It is just the same with the work of an artist of genius: this gives art a new impulse which changes it decisively: from then on it is no longer the same. I am tempted to say that the artist is immortal to the extent that he causes his contemporaries vexation, using that word in its biblical sense.'

'Then how do you explain the unchallengeable immortality of composers like Palestrina or Mozart or even Schubert, who in their own time made no alarming innovations of a kind that could have caused anybody vexation?'

'I am not so sure that Mozart was quite so meek and mild as people would have us believe. I don't think things were made easy for him, and, to put it baldly, I think he died in time to be regarded as just about a promising young composer, leaving out of account the countless failures that he experienced with his works. Schubert was known to only a relatively small circle of people and, as you pointed out earlier, many of his greatest works were known not even to those. Palestrina was perhaps the one great composer who strove for nothing but perfection and compliance with a stylistic tradition. The question might be raised whether some of his fame might not be due to the propaganda of subsequent conformists who were, no doubt, only too happy to see real greatness combined with apparent compliance.'

'For a philosopher you have an amazing insight into musical history.'

'If I had not, you would presumably not have come to me with your problems.'

'So you believe that in order to become immortal an artist must create something unprecedented, must shock his contemporaries to the core?'

'I would not like to maintain that such an attitude would assure him immortality. I have no prescription for immortality, and I don't think that any exists. I can only say that whoever takes a chance has a chance. If he stakes everything—himself, his spiritual and even if necessary his physical existence—he can win a great deal. And when Providence rewards him with the consciousness of having lost all, then he is in a state to gain all.'

'You realise that this is not the solution to my problem?'

'Did you really expect one? All I wanted to achieve by this conversation was to put you in a frame of mind in which you would permit me turn on the radio and listen with philosophic detachment to Benny Goodman's rippling clarinet. May I?'

ACKNOWLEDGEMENTS

On Writing My Memoirs; *Berkeley*, June 1951

A Puppet Play; *Die Szene*, September 1929

A Few Words about Johann Strauss; *'Die Oper'*, *Blätter des Breslauer Stadttheaters*, 1929/30

From *Jonny* to *Orest*; *Leipziger Neueste Nachrichten*, January 1930

Darius Milhaud; *Anbruch*, April/May 1930

Composing as a Calling; *Die Musikpflege*, September 1930

New Humanity and Old Objectivity; *Neue Schweizer Rundschau*, April 1931

The Freedom of the Human Spirit; *Anbruch*, January 1932

The Prolonged Funeral Banquet; *Anbruch*, April/May 1932

What Should Music Criticism Do?; *'23'*, *Eine Wiener Musikzeitschrift*, February 1933

Nationality and Art; *Neue Zürcher Zeitung*, January 1934

Karl Kraus and Arnold Schoenberg; *'23'*, *Eine Wiener Musikzeitschrift*, October 1934

On the Status of Western Music; *Wiener Zeitung*, February/March 1936

Is Opera Still Possible Today?; *Sonderdruck*, 1936

Alban Berg's *Lulu*; *Wiener Zeitung*, June 1937

Notes on Kafka's Collected Works; *Wiener Zeitung*, October 1937

Basic Principles of a New Theory of Musical Aesthetics; *Über neue Musik*, Verlag der Ringbuchhandlung, Wien 1937

Music of Eternity; *Basler Nachrichten*, November 1938

The Ivory Tower; *Music*, November 1944

The Composer and the Interpreter; *Black Mountain College Bulletin*, November 1944

That Noise Called Music; manuscript, 1945

Why 'Pallas Athene Weeps'; *Hamburgische Staatsoper*, 1955

The Libretto Problem; *Forum*, April 1956

What Electronic Music Is and How it is Made; *Forum*, September 1956

On the Ageing and Obsolescence of Music; *Forum*, December 1956

Conversation Past Midnight; manuscript, 1945